What Southern Women Know About

Flirting

The Fine Art of Social, Courtship, and Seductive Flirting to Get the Best Things in Life

A PERIGEE BOOK

WHAT SOUTHERN WOMEN KNOW ABOUT *Flirting*

RONDA RICH

A Perigee Book
Published by the Penguin Group
Penguin Group (USA) Inc.
375 Hudson Street, New York, New York 10014, USA
Penguin Group (Canada), 10 Alcorn Avenue, Toronto, Ontario M4V 3B2,
Canada
(a division of Pearson Penguin Canada Inc.)
Penguin Books Ltd., 80 Strand, London WC2R 0RL, England
Penguin Group Ireland, 25 St. Stephen's Green, Dublin 2, Ireland (a division of
Penguin Books Ltd.)
Penguin Group (Australia), 250 Camberwell Road, Camberwell, Victoria 3124,
Australia (a division of Pearson Australia Group Pty. Ltd.)
Penguin Books India Pvt. Ltd., 11 Community Centre, Panchsheel Park, New
Delhi—110 017, India
Penguin Group (NZ), cnr. Airborne and Rosedale Roads, Albany, Auckland
1310, New Zealand (a division of Pearson New Zealand Ltd.)
Penguin Books (South Africa) (Pty.) Ltd., 24 Sturdee Avenue, Rosebank,
Johannesburg 2196, South Africa

Penguin Books Ltd., Registered Offices: 80 Strand, London WC2R 0RL,
England

This book is an original publication of The Berkley Publishing Group.

Copyright © 2005 by Ronda Rich Creative, Inc.
Text design by Tiffany Estreicher

PERIGEE is a registered trademark of Penguin Group (USA) Inc.

ISBN: 0-399-53096-7

First edition: May 2005

This book has been cataloged by the Library of Congress

10 9 8 7 6 5 4 3 2

Most Perigee Books are available at special quantity discounts for bulk purchases
for sales promotions, premiums, fund-raising or educational use. Special books,
or book excerpts, can also be created to fit specific needs.

For details, write: Special Markets, The Berkley Publishing Group, 375 Hudson
Street, New York, New York 10014.

For Miss Virgie, Queen of Southern Flirts
and
Debbie, Queen of Best Friends

CONTENTS

INTRODUCTION
Isn't She Just Precious?   1

CHAPTER ONE
Flirt Alert   11

CHAPTER TWO
Flirting with Success   21

SOCIAL FLIRTING

CHAPTER THREE
Flirting 101   37

CHAPTER FOUR
Goodwill Comes to Those Who Wink   65

CHAPTER FIVE
Charmancity   77

CHAPTER SIX
Return on Assets: The Business of Flirting   89

COURTSHIP FLIRTING

CHAPTER SEVEN
The Belle Rings and Romance Answers   107

CHAPTER EIGHT
Scoring with Sports   129

CHAPTER NINE
Honeysuckle Kisses and Blackberry Cobblers   143

SEDUCTIVE FLIRTING

CHAPTER TEN
Luring Him in with Sweet Allure   157

CHAPTER ELEVEN
Rule the Roost, but Pamper the Rooster   169

CHAPTER TWELVE
The Fine Art of Winning His Heart with Red Silk
and Black Lace   177

Weekend Diary of a Flirt   187
Flirting at a Glance   199
Acknowledgments   209
About the Author   211

ISN'T SHE JUST PRECIOUS?

"Hello?" was barely out of my mouth when my friend Cynthia, born and raised in New York City, began babbling excitedly over the phone. Intercom voices boomed loudly in the background, telling me immediately that she was in an airport.

"Guess what!" she screamed above the noise. "I used your flirting advice and it worked! I got upgraded on my flight from LAX to New York!" Cross-country upgrades are, as we say in the South, as scarce as hen's teeth. Cynthia, a self-proclaimed neophyte at flirting, had read the first draft of the manuscript for this book. She rarely bothers with flirtation but, on a whim, she decided to practice it and see if it would land her a first-class accommodation.

"I didn't even recognize myself," she hurried on, reveling in her success. "I just did what you said to do. I was so sweet and charming. And it worked! If it can work for me, it can work for anyone."

Of course flirting works. And why wouldn't it? After all, flirting is simply the art of being real nice which, in turn, makes others feel good about themselves *and* about you. People mirror our treatment of them—good or bad. Going out of your way to be nice and courteous to others will yield favorable treatment for you. When others like us, they take joy in doing things for us. It's so simple but so often over-looked. *Nice*. It's a synonym, plain and simple, for flirting. It can be used personally, professionally and socially. It is appropriate—with certain guidelines—for use any place, any time, on any person. A good flirt sprinkles "feel good" magic dust over others and, as a result, reaps benefits and special favors.

In my first book, *What Southern Women Know (That Every Woman Should)*, I wrote one chapter on the art of flir-tation as practiced by Southerners. Reporters for well-known newspapers and magazines wrote articles, using that chapter and me as expert sources, and everyday women, who had shunned the idea of flirting as frivolous, gave it a try. Very often, to their surprise, it worked exceeding well.

"You know that stuff that Ronda wrote in her book about flirting?" an eighty-year-old friend of my mother's asked her. The woman, widowed for a couple of years, had caught the eye of a widower in her retirement home. "Well, I've been practicing everything she says to do and it works! I've got him wrapped around my finger. I hadn't flirted since I was a young girl and I had forgotten how. So, I just followed all her ad-vice." Pretty soon, those two were as thick as honey that's been setting in the jar too long, and Mama's eighty-year-old friend was giddy with girlish excitement.

Obviously, I didn't invent flirting, but I do think the women of the South perfected it. I recall asking a reporter from a major newspaper in Washington, D.C., why she was interviewing me about the art of flirtation. She laughed and replied, "Because everyone knows that Southern women are the *best* flirts."

I agree. Southern women know how to flirt. It comes as natural to us as the dew that falls across Dixie on a summer morning. Wisely, we use it to seduce both man and life into our sweet little hands. We make no apology for the potency of our charming, darling ways, for we long ago discovered that we could practice the ancient arts of femininity while proclaiming a strong-willed independence.

We are feminine feminists. We took the best from the worlds of our genteel, old-fashioned upbringing and the strong, visionary liberators of the women's movement to forge a brand of womanhood that is both gentle and strong. In that paradox of attributes lays an allure that is as undeniably refreshing as a cold glass of sweet tea on a broiling hot July afternoon after a few hours of sidewalk strolling in New Orleans.

But you don't have to have a Southern pedigree to master the art of being irresistible.

Every woman, Southern or not, was born to flirt.

Is there a better flirt than a toddler who can smear the cabinets with raspberry jam then smile so coquettishly, looking up through her eyelashes, that all is quickly forgiven? Her mischievous, spirited behavior quickly becomes delighted merriment to those around her who recognize the joy she brings. Think about the little girls who prance into the living room, climb up on Daddy's knee, straighten their prissy petti-coats, throw their arms around his neck, press a nose against his cheek, and begin with, "Daddy, I love you so much." His heart melts, and he responds lovingly. After a couple of min-utes of hugs and kisses, she then says, "Can I have a puppy dog?" If she doesn't get it then, she'll keep coming back with the same technique—flirting all the way—until she does.

Too many women grow up and grow out of this natural in-stinct. They discard it as carelessly as it a piece of junk mail—and in doing so, they sabotage future success.

Why?

It all boils down to the word *serious*. People become too serious-minded about life and forget to have fun while ac-complishing goals and winning hearts. In the South, though, we know what is truly serious in life because we are a region that has survived war, devastation that laid our land to waste, death, poverty, and famine. But the women of the Southern re-gion are always mighty serious about one thing—flirting. We don't take it lightly. We take it to heart.

The biggest misconception is that there is only one type of flirting—the whimsical, oh-what-big-muscles-you-have kind. Nothing is further from reality. Flirting, as you will discover, can be divided into three major categories: *Social, courtship*, and *seductive*. Used in varying degrees with certain guidelines in each category, flirting can lead you to find the ideal man, the perfect job, and fulfilling social life while bringing you wonder-ful little extras like airline upgrades. More often than not, it is not sexual, just friendly and warm and can be used with other women as well as men. In the workplace, it is not low-cut, bosom-brushing-against-the-arm flirtation but environment-appropriate thoughtfulness and appreciation. A wink is never out of place because it signifies approval, humor, and an invitation to come closer emotionally. A well-placed wink can be the perfect punctuation to a comment, question, or story.

My friend Susan, a Memphis debutante, has never worked a job but she knows how to work things to her advantage. She is a flirt extraordinaire, a trait that definitely impacts the bottom line of her family's budget. Here's one example: Her husband, Drew, had gotten three quotes for the repainting of the outside of their house. He was close to making a decision when Susan asked about the prices.

"They're all within a couple of hundred dollars of each other, so I'm going to take the middle one," he explained.

She plopped her elbows down on the kitchen counter and studied the estimates closely. Then she smiled, looked up at him, and winked. "I can get a better price."

He laughed. First mistake. "No, you can't." Second mistake. Never use that horrid four-letter word *can't* with a Southern woman.

She lifted one well-sculpted eyebrow and asked, "Whatta you wanna bet?"

He rolled his eyes. "This is ridiculous. Susan, I have spent two weeks on this and I know what I'm doing."

"No, you don't. You're a lawyer," she replied. "What makes you know more about painting than I do?"

Drew knew it was useless to argue and too time-consuming because once Susan starts, she doesn't quit. "Okay. Go ahead. Give it your best shot."

"And if I win?"

"I'll cook dinner every night for a week. Know what I want if I win?"

"Yes." She nodded confidently, knowing that he wanted what every man wants. "Sex every day for a week and twice on Saturday and Sunday."

He nodded happily, thinking how much he was going to enjoy winning.

She winked slyly. "And if you lose, in addition to cooking dinner, *no* sex for a week." She tossed that in, knowing that would really get him where it hurt. She didn't want to merely claim victory; she wanted the triumph to be unforgettable. They shook hands on it and Susan quickly got down to business.

She called friends and paint stores for recommendations and carefully researched until she was quite knowledgeable about house painting. After studious deliberation, she made a list of three names and called the first one on the list to make an appointment. Then she made her own appointments for manicure, pedicure, and hair in order to look her best. She knew it was important to make a good impression, plus she wanted to maximize her confidence, both of which are critical in such situations.

When the painter and his helper arrived, they were greeted by a lovely, feminine creature who was soft and innocent looking and very nonintimidating. The guards of caution dropped immediately. Putting forth her best social flirting techniques—and never coming close to anything remotely inappropriate—Susan showed them around her beloved home. She talked of family, asked about theirs, and reminisced of the good times shared by her children in the home. She carefully steered away from price. When the tour had ended, she said, "I just baked a pecan pie. It's still warm from the oven. Why don't you come in and have a cup of coffee and a piece of pie?"

Of course, they accepted. What man in his right mind would turn down that kind of hospitable offer? After warm pecan pie à la mode and coffee, Susan said sweetly with a smile, "Well, I suppose now has come the time to ask what your price would be." She put a hand to her forehead and said, "And please be gentle. I'm so afraid to ask."

He cleared his throat and waited a moment before naming a price significantly less than any quote that her husband had gotten. She knew better than to leap for joy, though.

"Well, I guess that would be okay but, actually, I was hoping for a couple of hundred dollars less." She punctuated the remark with a hopeful smile.

He sighed. "How 'bout we split the difference and do it for a hundred less?"

Like a wise woman, she stopped while she was ahead. No sense wasting effort and charm, so she agreed, and canceled the other two appointments.

While the painters were working on the house, Susan plied them with Southern hospitality, toting lemonade and home-made cookies to them, and chatting amicably. The painters were so grateful that they painted her daughter's playhouse in the backyard at no additional charge. Isn't she just precious? That's what we Southern women like to say about others who impress us. It's a trademark Southern woman compliment.

As for Drew, it's hard to say which price was higher for him—cooking for a week or no sex for seven days. Though, I think we women all know the answer to that one.

A good friend, Sarah Anne, is a well-known media personality in Nashville. That girl can slap-dab flirt with the best of them, something she was good at even before she upgraded her bra by a size or two. Whenever she takes her children to the grocery store to buy fresh fish, the manager of the seafood department gets on the P.A. system and announces her presence in the store. Then he pulls out wriggling lobsters to the delight of her children and entertains them joyfully.

"Which means, being Southern and kind, I feel I need to hug him with all his fish juices and slime running down his white smock, thinly disguised with Polo cologne," she explains. "It never fails that I take home fresh fish at half the cost of other customers who don't give him a second look or hug a man who smells like the bottom of the sea."

Isn't she just precious?

In business, flirting is as important as a good calculator and dictionary. Many folks I work with professionally often hear, "I adore you! Thank you so much. What would I ever do without you?" or "Oh, darling one! How I desperately need your help!" When a couple of those guys heard there was going to be this book on flirting, I received emails from them. One said: "I believe that I have, indeed, been on the receiving end of some of that flirting. And, to be honest, I have quite enjoyed it."

Another wrote, "It's easy to see how we men can think we're in charge when dealing with Southern women like you. When, actually, we're just putty in your hands."

You, too, were born to flirt.

No doubt you were well accomplished at it when you were three. But just how good are you now? And how can you get your flirting techniques back into tip-top shape? Read on to find out.

CHAPTER ONE

FLIRT ALERT

You know her. You can spot her the moment she enters a room. She may not be beautiful, but she will certainly be dynamic, drawing to her both men and women. She has presence. She is warm, friendly, sparkling with the joy of life and has an effervescence that springs forth from a strong self-confidence.

In many cases, she is self-made, carefully hand-knitted into the alluring, flirtatious woman she has become. Sometimes, she is overtly solicitous and warm. Other times, her flirtation is quiet but powerful, drawing others to her subliminally. Sometimes, she is dressed flamboyantly while other times, she will be the one in the most understated outfit. Still, by her flirtatious aura, you will know her.

"I have someone I want you to meet," a friend said to me at a speaking event. He went on to explain who she was and that she was a powerful executive. He then concluded with, "She is

so lovely." To be called "lovely" is one of the strongest compliments in the world. It speaks solidly of a gentle, soothing,
extremely likeable person. When she arrived, he brought over
a plain woman dressed in a drab, ill-fitted suit with too-long
sleeves. Her self-confidence and warm, courteous manner,
however, made her beautiful and alluring. I was captivated by
the sparkle in her green eyes and the subtle manner with
which she socially flirted. She was, indeed, lovely; a well-
trained social flirt who had climbed the corporate ladder of
success in a pair of sensible heels rather than a pair of Manolo
Blahnik stilettos. Besides smarts and talent, she had used expert social flirting skills to work her way to the top. She was
warm and welcoming from the moment she said, "Hello." She
made me feel good about myself because she made me feel important and deserving of her time. A week or so after the introduction, I received the loveliest, handwritten note from this
busy executive who took the time to be gracious to a new acquaintance. I was impressed because it was obvious that she is
a master at social flirting.

FLIRT ALERT:

Be your own best friend. Believe in your best and
you will become your best.

An accomplished flirter is buoyed by steely self-confidence.
Flirting sometimes leads to love. However, love always leads to
flirting because to excel at it, you must first fall in love with the
most important person in your universe: Yourself. I learned
this from a friend in Little Rock, who is an incredible flirt.

"What makes you such a good flirt?" I asked after watching her in action at a charity ball.

"I'm completely in love." She smiled teasingly then winked. "With myself. I like myself so much that I am absolutely convinced that others will, too." Her delightful laughter rang out merrily then her look became serious. "People who don't like themselves or suffer from low self-esteem aren't excited about introducing themselves to others. That reluctance shows and pushes others away."

Here's the best advice on that: *Stay away from others who chip away at your self-confidence.* You know the ones. They're artful at slicing your Achilles tendon with a quick dig and then looking horrified that you didn't take it as a joke. Don't let them kid you. They meant it. Sometimes that's your mother. Mothers can say the worst things to their daughters, things your worst enemies wouldn't even dare think.

"I wouldn't change a thing about you," one friend's mother said to her in a sweet, tearful moment that lasted only briefly. "Well, I would have you lose five pounds." She stepped back and looked at her daughter ruefully. "Maybe ten."

Families can be brutal with comments. Work at tossing off these negative comments, as well as not giving them yourself. If you practice seeing the positive in others, you'll also see it in yourself. You can distance yourself from friends who throw barbs in your direction but, of course, it's harder with family. You have to learn to turn a deaf ear to such words. Besides, if you're beat up in the bosom of your family and can deal with it, it is great training for the outside world.

My sister was a precocious little girl with green eyes and lots of tumbling blond curls. Mama always dressed her three little girls in frills and lots of petticoats, so we were often eye-catching. But with my sister, friends would always talk about how cute she was and how much she looked just like our daddy, while my other sister and I looked like Mama. One day, Mama walked into the bedroom and found her three-year-old staring with great admiration at herself in the mirror.

"I'm just the cutest little thing," my sister was saying to her reflection. "I look just like my daddy!"

We can all learn from that. *Take the positive comments from others to heart and toss away the negative ones.* Though it's always necessary to seek improvement, keep a healthy attitude about it. Don't beat yourself up over weight you need to lose. Better yourself by doing it. Every time you dress, stand in front of the mirror and say, "I'm smart. I'm talented. I'm beautiful. I'm interesting and others will be intrigued by what I have to say." Give constant reinforcement to self-esteem-building comments by repeating them over and over to yourself while you bathe, clean house, walk your dog, drive to work, wait in store lines, or prepare dinner. There are lots of moments in the day when you can take important time to be kind to yourself and lay blocks that will lead you to build a better existence for yourself. As you're falling asleep at night, fill your mind with positive thoughts about yourself, your life, and your ambitions. While you sleep, these thoughts will sink deep into your subconscious and become a built-in compass for directing you on a positive path of flirting success.

Do You Pass the Test?

So, are you the kind of woman who sends out an all-points Flirt Alert when you enter a room? Let's see if the numbers add up:

Discover Your Flirting I.Q.

1. *You believe that flirting is appropriate to use*
   A. In any situation.
   B. Only socially.
   C. Never.

2. *Your self-confidence is based on*
   A. Your healthy opinion and the positive encouragement of others.
   B. Your opinion and the criticisms of others.
   C. Everything negative that your mother ever said.

3. *You flirt with*
   A. Everyone, including other women, children, and dogs.
   B. Select guys, especially the cute ones.
   C. No one. You tried it and didn't like it.

4. *Conversationally, you are able to discuss*
   A. Tidbits on a wide variety of topics.
   B. The latest fashion wars among design houses.
   C. Office and neighborhood gossip.

5. *At parties, you feel comfortable*
   A. Always.
   B. Sometimes.
   C. Never.

6. *When choosing an outfit for a big event, you always*
   A. Select the color and style that makes you feel terrific.
   B. Call all your friends to see what they're wearing and get their approval.
   C. Choose black because it's safe.

7. *You believe that your best accessory is*
   A. A friendly, bright smile.
   B. A pair of gold earrings.
   C. A pair of natural-colored Jimmy Choos.

8. *On a plane, if you sit next to a stranger, you will*
   A. Strike up a conversation and make a new friend.
   B. Smile, say hello, then turn your attention to a book or magazine.
   C. Never acknowledge the person and turn in your seat so that you're facing away.

9. *If you got a promotion, you would*
   A. Take your boss to lunch as a thank you.
   B. Shake her hand and thank her personally.
   C. Be too shy to mention it.

10. *If you admired another woman for her beauty or outfit but you didn't know her, you would*

A. March right over and tell her.

B. Smile and nod if she looked in your direction but never approach her.

C. Avoid contact of any kind.

11. *When you need to pick up your spirits and feel better about yourself, you*

A. Treat yourself to an expensive pair of sexy high heels.

B. Watch a favorite movie.

C. Indulge in a carton of your favorite ice cream.

12. *If you saw your boss's husband at a party, you would*

A. Be cordial, chatty but not flirtatious.

B. Say hello, shake hands, and move on.

C. Ignore him completely.

13. *When a colleague has a success, you*

A. Send a note of congratulations, flowers, or both.

B. Verbally acknowledge it when you run into her.

C. Never mention it.

14. *If you were dining with girlfriends and saw a guy who caught your attention, you would*

A. Strike up a conversation by asking how he liked the salmon because you're "thinking of ordering the same thing."

B. Keep looking in his direction and smile whenever you caught his eye.

C. Say nothing and avoid any eye contact.

15. *When you go out with a terrific guy, you*
    A. Make certain that he knows that you like him then wait for him to pursue you.
    B. Let the chips fall by themselves, however they will fall.
    C. Call or e-mail him repeatedly.

16. *On a first date, you would kiss him good night*
    A. Never.
    B. Sometimes.
    C. Always.

17. *By the fifth date, you would sleep with him*
    A. Never.
    B. Maybe.
    C. Definitely.

18. *To you, matching lingerie is*
    A. Definitely a necessity of life.
    B. Used only for special occasions.
    C. Bare is better.

19. *When you find yourself in a relationship, you*
    A. Pamper him but keep your power.
    B. Give yourself up for whatever he wants and take nothing.
    C. Do nothing for him and expect royal treatment in return.

20. *When you run into a difficult situation, you are most likely to*

    A. Use persistence, charm, and ingenuity until you overcome it.

    B. Give a decent try before leaving it alone.

    C. Hand it off to someone else.

Determine your score by counting your A responses. If you got 20 A's, you should have written this book yourself! If you got 16–19, start a flirting support group and help others; 12–15, you have strong potential, but you could learn a thing or two; 7–11, there's hope; 6 or less: there's no time to waste—let's get to work immediately!

CHAPTER TWO

FLIRTING WITH SUCCESS

It takes a smart woman to flirt. A good flirt is a thinking woman who is articulate, clever, quick-witted, and well-versed on many subjects. The most successful flirts are also thoughtful, kindhearted, friendly, and unfailingly gracious. Women are born to flirt, but the best flirts are self-made because they take that natural instinct and fine-tune it to perfect pitch.

Southern women have long been considered experts on this artistry that comes as natural to us as the moss that hangs from the mighty oaks of Charleston and Savannah. Why? Because the South is a very open-armed, hands-on culture where, according to legend, the warmth of the climate spills over into the personalities of its people. Folks like warmth. They like a straight-in-the-eye look, a welcoming smile, engaging touch or an embrace, a tone of voice that is friendly, and thoughtful gestures that make them feel good. Southerners, both men and women, are unsurpassed in their abilities to tie all that together and employ it to the extent that the recipient is charmingly mesmerized. From these interactions, friendships are born, business relationships are created, and romances are ignited. While both genders of Southerners, due to the region's storied graciousness, are born with a natural proclivity for flirting, the South's women have the art down to finely manicured perfection.

What Is Flirting?

Flirting is a personal interaction that is fun, playful, lighthearted, and extremely productive in creating and enhancing relationships. Its greatest attraction is that it is never mean-spirited or unkind. It spreads a feeling of goodwill and good humor as steadily as kudzu spreads on a warm summer's day. For those who might not know about the potency of kudzu, it is a green leafy plant that covers a million acres of Southern soil and grows at the rate of 100 feet per season. It's impossible to control. Just like the charms of an irresistible flirt.

FLIRT ALERT:

The best flirt is always the one having the most fun.

FLIRTING IS POWER

In a world of feminists and modern day female independence, is flirting old-fashioned? Yep, it sure is. But look how well it worked for Eve, Bathsheba, Cleopatra, Mata Hari, and Mae West. Flirting is like a toothbrush. It's hard to improve on something so simple that has worked so well for centuries. Basically, I still use the same kind of toothbrush that my great-grandmother used, and I still flirt like she did. There have been only a few tweaks here and there. The big mistake that has been made in the last few decades is that too many women have moved away from flirting because they feared men would not take them seriously. Ha! In trying to gain serious-minded power, those who chose to follow that course, ironically, gave up their greatest power.

Flirting is a woman's most valuable weapon—with both men and women. It's the one that is given naturally to every woman and has been since God created woman. The same men who rebel against tough-acting women in the corporate world and will fight them without courtesy will melt into a mushy puddle from a kind word and a flirtatious smile. A good definition for flirting: The time-honored technique of making others feel good about themselves *and* about you. We Southern women proudly practice it without shame or hesitation. Besides being so productive, it's also much less stressful than being mean and uptight! Charm, a key component of flirting, disarms even the toughest ones. In the pages that follow, we'll carefully explore flirting in three categories: *social, courtship,* and *seductive.* Each one is important to master if you want to attract the very best in life.

FLIRT ALERT:

A feminine feminist finds power in flirting and uses it whenever she needs to.

IT'S SO BASIC

The basic elements of flirting are the same in each category, but are intensified at each level. It's like making a mint julep. A little bourbon in the mint julep makes for a relaxed, fun, laughter-filled time. Increasing the amount of bourbon a bit more turns up the warmth and fun, and making the drink even stronger is a recipe for a good time to be had by all. Thus is the case with flirting as it progresses from social to courtship to seductive.

Social flirting is appropriate to use in any situation, including professional situations. It is an invaluable networking tool in making new friends and strengthening bonds with old friends. It's also outrageously helpful in getting those precious little favors that makes life more pleasant—airline and hotel upgrades, backstage invitations, hard-to-get restaurant reservations, discounts on merchandise, moving to the front of the line, and on and on. Professionally, it works terrifically and can, in fact, lead to promotions, big sales, and a network of contacts that opens doors.

Social flirting was patented and raised to glorious heights by Southerners. It is emotionally enticing and spiritually soothing but not physically seductive. Since it works as well on the same gender as it does on the opposite sex, it should also be known as the art of coaxing life into the palm of your pretty, little hand.

One night, a friend of mine, an Alabama-trained diva, and her husband left a Christmas party and immediately entered into an argument over her allure and charm, which had held most of the men at the party captivated. He thought she had taken too far her vow to always uphold social flirting as a critical attribute of Southern womanhood. As they argued, he swerved the car and looked up moments later to see a blue light flashing behind them. He pulled over and a trooper approached the car. Since my friend's husband, an attorney, had partaken of a couple of glasses of wine over the course of the evening, he was a bit nervous. After checking his license, the trooper said, "Sir, can you recite the alphabet for me?"

My friend leaned across her husband and said sweetly with a flutter of her eyelashes, "Now, officer, he couldn't recite the alphabet when he was a senior at Ole Miss. *Why* would you expect that of him *now*?" She finished the question with a delicious, flirtatious smile, and the officer laughed so hard that he dropped the whole matter. As her chastised husband pulled the car back onto the road, she asked mischievously, *"Now*, what do you *think* of my charm?"

Courtship flirting is the demure, feminine science of sweetly attracting a man until he falls madly and inescapably in love. Unfortunately, in today's society, there is a trend to move into intimacy too quickly, which can savagely sabotage long-term commitment. Fires of passion that are started slowly, using flirtation as the kindling, burn hotter and longer. It's human nature to want something more when there's been a long, tantalizing period of anticipation. Courtship flirting is about making love and romance endure the passage of time. It is also about enticing the guy with cleverness and smarts.

Julianna called one day. "You've got to help me! You've got to help me!" she chattered excitedly the moment I answered the phone.

My heart sped up. "What's wrong?" I answered, scared by the urgency of her tone.

"Richard called me and asked me for a date!"

That explained it. Julianna had been carrying a torch for Richard since the first grade, when she used to trail behind him on the playground. In high school, it was an annual ritual of mourning when he asked—as he always did—someone else to the homecoming dances and proms. Newly divorced, Richard was now back on the market and, at last, after twenty-five years of dedicated worship, Julianna had her chance. We had to plan carefully for it. They were going to dinner. So, the plotting began. I knew that Richard was a race fan. I also knew that Julianna didn't know a racecar from a pace car.

"Are you willing to do whatever it takes, to catch his fancy?" I asked.

"Yes," she replied firmly. "As long as it's legal and moral, or mostly so."

"You need to learn about racing."

"Anything but *that!*" she retorted. "I hate sports. Yuck."

"Okay," I replied. "This is your big chance and you're going to blow it." It took some convincing but finally she agreed to play along. I made up a simple list of facts and trivia about the sport for her to memorize.

"Throw these out from time to time in the conversation," I instructed.

"What if he asks me more than this?"

I laughed. "He won't. Once you get a man started about sports or a favorite subject, he takes over."

To her credit, she listened and Richard was impressed. So much so that he asked her for another date. Then, it became a regular Sunday afternoon date, watching the races together. Soon she understood the sport and even halfway liked it. Perhaps it was coincidence, but shortly after a trip to the Daytona 500—she gave him the tickets for Christmas—he proposed. Personally, I don't think there was any coincidence to it. I think it was a perfectly executed strategy in the game of courtship flirting.

After courtship flirting, a relationship will move naturally toward *seductive flirting*. In the beginning, as we all know, the playfulness of seductive flirting comes without thought or planning. As the relationship ages or other factors such as stress and children come along, it's a matter of putting the fun back into it. *Remember:* Flirting in any form is fun including seductive flirting where the key word is *playfulness*.

Women fall in love with our hearts and from what we hear a man say to us. Which is why smooth-talking guys can cut a wide swath through a big ol' pasture of love-starved women. Men, though, are a bit more shallow because they fall in love with what they *see*. Appearances are important to them. In seductive flirting, what they see is what they'll want—or not want. From the first date to the celebration of your fiftieth wedding anniversary, dress in the way that appeals to him, even when it takes more effort. In the long run, it will pay off. Secondly, men are attracted by fragrance. Next to how she *looks*, the way a woman *smells* is her most seductive weapon in the battle of the sexes.

One day over lunch, Katie Anne confided that her husband loved the new fragrance she had purchased one day while we were shopping.

"That perfume drives him crazy!" Astonished, she rolled her big blue eyes. "I dab a bit on every afternoon before he comes home from work and I'll tell you this—he practically crushes me by kissing and hugging me so tight."

"You know what you should do?" I asked, spearing a piece of lettuce. "The next time he goes on a business trip, spray a handkerchief with the fragrance, drop it into a tightly sealed plastic bag and hide it among his clothes." I winked. "He'll really be going by the time he gets home."

She did and, sure enough, he was crazed with passion by the time he got home. He told Katie Anne that he kept taking the handkerchief out and sniffing it. He even slept with it next to his pillow. "It's a good thing that I got some extra rest while he was gone," she explained. "Because I sure didn't get any that first night when he got home!"

Putting It in Play

My godmother called in distress one Sunday afternoon to say that she was going to be late for a tea party at my house, if she was even able to come at all. She hates to miss a party so I knew something big was up. As it turned out, something big was down: A huge, hundred-year-old oak tree had fallen across her driveway, hitting a power line as it fell. An emergency power company crew was on its way over to cut it away from the electrical lines.

When she finally arrived for the tea, she explained that all had turned out well. The power company guys had completely cut up the big tree and promised to return the following day to haul it off.

I was perplexed. "The power company cut up the entire tree, *and* they're coming back to remove it?"

She chuckled in a delighted, self-satisfied way. "That's right."

Puzzled, I shook my head. "That's unusual. Normally, they just cut away the part of the tree that's on the line."

She grinned. "That's what my neighbor said. He said that when one of his trees fell, the power company cut the limb away from the electrical lines, then he had to hire someone else to come in and cut up the tree and remove it." She paused then winked. "But I guess that *he* didn't invite the crew in for homemade cake and coffee."

That explained it. She's the greatest baker I know. "Was it fresh coconut cake?" I asked.

"Sure was."

I shivered with admiration. "Well, in that case, they'll probably be back to mow your yard all summer!"

In the South, we staunchly believe that if you can't charm 'em, just feed 'em. *The greatest tool for flirting, especially social flirting, is food.* Men aren't the only ones who can be swayed by a delicious dish. In cupboards across the South, you'll find an assortment of casserole dishes, pie plates, Tupperware cake carriers, and deviled egg platters. It's part of the arsenal in our war to charmingly disarm and socially engage. You can always detect Southern blood in a woman's DNA if she has at least five recipes that call for cream of mushroom soup, she makes deviled eggs for every special occasion, and has dishes with masking tape on the bottom with her name written on it. That means, of course, she's been taking good-will casseroles to the ill and bereaved. It may also mean she's running for president of the PTA and has been using her best social flirting skills to sway votes.

Shortly after my godmother's experience, a tree fell in the woodsy area behind my house. I called a couple of tree surgeons and discovered it would cost a few hundred dollars to remove it. One afternoon, I noticed that my neighbor was having some trees removed. I went over and asked if he would bring one of the crew to my house so I could get an estimate. I had just finished dressing for a birthday party—my outfit was close to adorable—and was getting ready to leave when the doorbell rang. My neighbor introduced me to the guy, and I immediately set about socially flirting, grateful that I was unexpectedly but appropriately attired for the mission at hand. *Serious social flirting calls for your Sunday best.* I thanked him profusely for taking the time to come over and, as we walked around back to look at the tree, I explained how hard these things are to handle when you aren't married.

"I just don't know anything at all about these things," I explained, shaking my head sadly. "And none of the men I know is smart enough to know anything about it either. Let me ask you something." I stopped and reached out to grasp his forearm. I looked him directly in the eyes. "What good is a wall filled with degrees if you don't even know how to program a VCR or, for heaven's sake, cut down a tree? Real men are disappearing rapidly from our society, and it's a crying shame." I dropped my head and shook it woefully.

He threw out his chest and swaggered down to the back of the yard. He scurried down to look at the fallen tree and returned in a couple of minutes. Shyly, he asked, "Would twenty be too much!"

"Twenty dollars?" I was astounded since the lowest estimate over the phone had been three hundred.

"That too much?" he asked with alarm.

"Are you going to haul it off for that?"

He shifted from one foot to the other. "Well, I wasn't plannin' on it."

"If I pay you forty dollars, will you haul it off?"

"Yes m'am!"

I wasted not one second, hurrying inside to get the money and a couple of books, which I signed for him. Signed with very sweet, gushing notes, I might add. By the way, that's another strong component of Southern hospitality and social flirting: When someone comes to visit, we always scrounge around to find something for them to take home with them. We believe it's the "neighborly" thing to do.

FACE-TO-FACE FLIRTING

Flirting works best in person so if it's a dire situation, powder up, perfume up, dress up, and show up to take on the situation with a personal touch. The previous estimates I had gotten for the tree removal had been over the phone. When I talked to someone in person, I got it done for hundreds of dollars less.

Flirting can, however, work effectively over the phone. It just calls for relying completely on clever conversation, wit, tone of voice, reliable research, and information—and a sensitivity to the other person's tone and reactions. Such was the case when the highway department slapped a speed limit sign smack in the middle of my front yard. First, I talked to the crew who was putting up the sign.

FLIRT ALERT:

Short skirts can create shortcuts to
problem-solving.

"It's out of our control," the foreman explained. "We have to put them exactly where the engineers tell us. They have laws about this." In my nicest, most desperate way, I begged for help. So, with a wink and an admonishment not to tell where I got it, he gave me the phone number for the highest-ranking boss.

"There is no way that you're going to get that sign moved," warned a friend, but he was a guy who didn't know the power behind flirtatious desperation. "It's a wasted a phone call."

I called the boss and began with chatty, friendly conversation. I told him who I was, where I lived, and how nice the crew was that worked on the project. Amicably, we discussed my neighborhood, traffic pattern, speed limits, and such. *The key in such situations is to establish friendly rapport.* It's much harder to say no to a nice person than it is to a mean one.

"Is it true that there are laws that dictate exactly where the signs should be placed?" *Ask questions because it shows respect to the person in charge.* Also, you'll gain favor because others enjoy sharing their knowledge and expertise.

"Yes," he replied. Then he began to explain the complication of the law that dictated that signs must be placed such and such distance from such and such place, the distance between signs should be precisely X amount, and so on. It was typical red tape but interesting, nonetheless, because who would have ever thought that a simple matter such as street signs had to subscribe to a complicated formula. With great friendliness, I continued to ask questions. After several questions and answers, he concluded, "So, apparently, the dimensions dictated by the law have placed the sign in your front yard."

I sighed deeply. To my new friend, I explained how bad the sign looked at the edge of my yard, then in a sad voice, I said, "I recently divorced, and I have to mow my own yard. It's been a difficult adjustment." I sighed heavily again. "I don't know how on earth I am going to mow it with that sign there."

"Oh, I see." His voice dropped. True gentlemen are chivalrous at heart. It's innate in their behavior. Despite society's pressure by some women who are plotting to disable the advantage of our womanhood and therefore making men wary of offering a hand, most men are still inclined to help a damsel in distress. Don't hesitate to use it as a trump card. The truth of the matter is we all need help at times. Face up to it and be honest about it. Besides, being brave takes too much energy.

I perked up a bit. "Is it *possible* that there has been a mismeasurement? That the sign actually belongs elsewhere?" *Another steadfast rule is to be smart, think quickly, and offer the other person a way out or a solution.*

I heard his voice brighten. "Maybe. Hmmm." He paused for a second. These are the times to hold your breath, whisper a prayer, and say not a single word. I waited. Then he spoke. "Tell you what. I'll come out there and oversee the remeasuring myself. Perhaps there *was* a problem in the calculation."

The next day, the crew's foreman rang my doorbell. He was grinning when I opened the door. "M'am, just thought I'd let you know that we're moving the sign."

I gasped in delight. "You are?" I clapped my hands happily. "Where?"

"About a hundred feet past your yard. I thought you'd be happy." He turned to go but looked back. "Darnedest thing I ever saw." He shook his head, his face covered with amusement. "I've been doing this job for twenty years and this is the first time we ever had a *miscalculation*. First time we ever got sent out to move a sign."

I shrugged it off. Never gloat to others when social flirting has proven successful. It isn't attractive. "Well, I'm certain that it wasn't your fault." I winked. "Must have been bad batteries in the calculator or something."

As he walked off, he chuckled and said under his breath, "Yeah. Bad batteries or something."

As this story illustrates, flirting is a wonderful gift. It is useful in networking, socializing, career advancement, matchmaking, lovemaking, and everyday tasks such as the repositioning of ugly traffic signs. And, like with all things, the more you practice, the better you get at it. So, let's get busy!

Social Flirting

CHAPTER THREE

FLIRTING 101

Anyone can flirt. At any age. You don't have to be eighteen or a size eight. You don't have to be beautiful. You don't have to be bursting with personality. You only have to possess the spark of desire and a sparkle in your eyes. It simply begins with a friendliness and openness that invites people to come closer. You don't have to be an extrovert to flirt. In fact, an introvert can use key elements of flirting to lure people across the room to her—without making a sound. Then all it takes is asking two or three perfect questions, and the conversation takes off. It's easy for even the shyest person.

The best flirts know that flirtation starts with playful repartee. It isn't serious or literal but rather it is a dance with words, winks, and smiles. An analytic who is accustomed to doing business in a boardroom has a hard time playing the game. I once dated someone who is smart, handsome, and a successful executive, yet I swear that man doesn't have a flirting bone in his body. If I were gone for a couple of days or simply hadn't talked to him in several hours, I would ask playfully on the phone, "Have you missed me?"

This is an opening line of flirtation I often use on guys I'm dating. The guys who play the game well, will say something like, "I sure have. I thought about that bright smile of yours all the time. Kept me awake at night thinking about it. Thought about your sweet kisses, too."

But this guy, *this* guy, bless his heart, couldn't play the game regardless of how many times I spelled out the rules. His response was either, "Well, yes. But to be honest, I've been so busy that I haven't had much time to think about missing you. But when I had time, I missed you." Or—and this one drove me nuts—"I'm not going to tell you that. Why would I tell you that?"

Regardless of what I asked in a flirtatious, teasing way, he responded with a serious, literal answer. Talk about doomed lovers! An Alabama football fan can marry an Auburn fan and produce better results than those produced when a flirter hooks up with a non-flirter. Even a cat and a dog are a better match than a flirter and non-flirter.

FLIRT ALERT:

There's power in a pucker, whether it's a pout or
a kiss.

A Primer on Flirting

The key elements of flirtation are simple, but a few take practice and one or two take a little work. Southern women, many born into regional subcultures where hard work is a given, excel at working and practicing, especially when it comes to one of our favorite pastimes.

Strong Self-Esteem

Some folks have good self-esteem because it was nurtured from early childhood in a family that made a conscious effort to instill it. Most of us have to learn it. That begins with knowing what makes us feel insecure, such as a lack of education or social skills, excess weight, or other insecurities. As a child, I was terribly self-conscious about an overbite. Braces, thankfully, changed that, and my self-esteem surged. In hindsight, if I had been given a choice of braces to straighten my teeth or a college education, braces would have won hands-down. My smile has definitely gotten me further than my degrees! The bottom line is that people are attracted to others who feel strong and good about themselves. If you don't like yourself, why should others? If there is something that bothers you about yourself such as crooked teeth, a bump on your nose, or bad skin, fix it. It'll be the best investment you ever make.

Irresistible Humor

Laughter is undeniably potent in drawing others to you. Napoleon once said, "A woman who laughs is a woman conquered." Now, if that little serious-minded bully recognized the allure of humor, that's a strong endorsement for its power. Southerners are renowned for our sense of humor, especially the self-effacing kind we use in our stories. In flirtation, a sense of humor will always be your greatest ally.

Not long ago I was tearing down a country side road, late for a photo shoot. As I came around a curve, I saw—too late— two law enforcement officers standing on the side of the road in what appeared to be a speed trap. One was holding a radar gun while the other was motioning offenders to pull over. Three cars were already sidelined, and with one wave of a hand, I became the fourth one. Due to the overcrowded situation, it was hard for me to get my car completely out of the road. The officer approached my car. He nodded and sternly said, "Hello, ma'am." With a nice smile and greeting, I handed him my license and insurance card. He looked at the back end of my car. "Ma'am, if you don't mind, could I get you to pull forward a little more? Your tail's sticking out in the road."

I couldn't resist. I pulled my sunglasses off, grinned and said, with a wink, "See?" I spread my upturned palms. "I have that problem all the time. My tail's always sticking out." I shook my head in comic puzzlement. Perfect. The self-effacing remark hit the mark and the officer threw back his head and laughed big. "I'll be right back," he said.

When he returned, he handed back my license and insurance card. "I'm gonna give you a warning but you're awful lucky because I've been writing tickets. So do me a favor and slow down. Okay?"

See what a little humor will do?

High-Heeled Hopes and Brightly Colored Spirits

Here is the core of flirtation: fun, frivolity, and filled with delightful humor. Don't take yourself or this game seriously. It ruins it. That means it's best to begin without any agenda such as: "I want to be the boss." "I want to marry this guy." "I want to be her friend." "I want him to help me with the class paper I'm working on." No strategies. No plans. No objectives. Just keep your spirits high and your heart light. In the beginning, keep it very simple and pure. The better you psych yourself up, the greater your chances for success will be. It needs to feel natural to you as well as to those around you.

Lighthearted and Playful Tone

Let the sound of your voice say it all. Clearly and loudly, it should say, "Let's have fun!" Others will feel favorable toward you, and the delightful journey will be under way. Let your voice sing, zing, and ring with irresistible playfulness. Your tone isn't the only one that's important. Listening carefully to how the other person says something is the main factor in gauging how the person is responding to you. As the other person's tone grows warmer, so can yours. Being alert to voice tone, especially over the phone, is one of the most helpful skills you will ever employ.

Spirit of Goodwill

Kindliness starts from deep inside and may require a little work, but this is truly what makes all flirting work. People respond to inner beauty quicker than they respond to outer looks. Southern mamas always warn their daughters, "Pretty is as pretty does." My niece, Nicole, who grew up to be a great beauty and a reluctant beauty queen—her mama entered her in pageants against her wishes—has always lived by those words. Once when she was about twelve years old, she confided to me that every night she prayed that God wouldn't let her grow up to be prettier than any of her friends. He didn't answer that one. She also prayed that she wouldn't have a big bosom like the other women in the family. That prayer was definitely answered.

Genuine Interest

Everyone has a story of some kind. Regardless of what it is, it is interesting because our stories make us who we are. Everyone has a skill or talent. By asking questions about another's life, skills, and talent, you gain insight into the individual and chances are you'll learn something. One night at a party, I started chitchatting with a stranger who turned out to be a floral designer. Southern women are renowned for flower arranging skills but, unfortunately, I'm not one of them. I jumped right on that and started asking for tips and information. She was delighted. "I'm so impressed that you're interested and want to know." As for me, I learned how to arrange flowers in a "ball" or "A." It was successful night for both of us.

Knowledge

Read. Read. Read. Observe and learn. It's that simple. Keep up with current events and pop culture. You never know when a piece of seemingly insignificant information will serve you well in a moment of flirtation. Many times I have worked a room by dropping a line here and there about everything from business news to sports to rock stars to Broadway plays. And, honestly, all I knew was a line about each but it was enough to get a conversation off and running.

I was at a Tupperware party at Nicole's house one evening when the sales lady announced that we were going to have a trivia contest.

I sat up straight, threw my shoulders back, and announced comically, "Well, if this is a trivia contest about Tupperware then *I* am going to win." I smiled confidently and thumped my chest. "Because I watched a documentary about Tupperware on PBS."

My sister, Louise, wrinkled her face into an expression of disbelief and shook her head. "Puh-leaze." She rolled her eyes. "*Who* would watch a *documentary* on *Tupperware?*"

Me. And that's why I won the trivia contest and made fast, new friends with the Tupperware lady. We bonded because I was reasonably well-versed on a subject that interested her.

Compliments Aplenty

You can't flirt without flattering. Can't be done! You have to make others feel good about themselves so that they feel good about you. Everyone, even the mean woman who lives next door, has something to compliment. I was at a reception following a speaking engagement I had done. While I was speaking, I noticed a woman in the audience who glared the entire time. No smile, no encouragement, nothing. At the reception I asked a mutual acquaintance about her and learned a little of her history. "She's a tough one," I was told. "She's not nice to anyone." I smiled and winked. "Well, watch this." I walked straight toward her and said, "That is the most beautiful outfit. I bet I know exactly what store it came from because that's where I buy my clothes." Her eyes lit up with pleasant surprise when I named the store. I was right. I just started oozing up to her and slowly her ice began to melt. She even turned warm. A good friend of mine, a Southern woman who is a flirt of the finest kind, came rushing up to hurry me along to dinner. Without knowing anything, she stopped, looked at the woman, and said, "You look beautiful! Love that outfit." Strong Southern women never hesitate to compliment other women. Approach the toughest person in the room and slather him or her with charm. Staying away from such people is like the gambler who walks away and leaves money on the table. You could be walking away from someone who could be very important to you. She could be a link to someone else you need to know or a wonderful opportunity and you would otherwise never find.

A longtime friend of mine—friends since the early days of our careers—is a powerful, successful sports executive. Because of our friendship, he agreed to do a luncheon speaking engagement for my sister, who was the program chair. She had never met him so I took him to her office before the event. She walked in, stopped dead in her tracks, and did a dramatic double take. He stood, introduced himself, and they shook hands. As he sat down, Louise walked around him to her desk, shaking her head. She smiled and looked at him for a few seconds. "I wasn't expecting someone so young and handsome." She was obviously taken aback because she admitted that she was expecting to meet someone older and not so dapper.

"I don't know why," she said. "But I guess I thought that you'd have to be much older to be in your position. Not a young, good-looking guy." She punctuated the remark by shaking her head again in astonishment.

She was genuine in her reaction and wasn't playing him. What she did, though, was be honest in a positive, complimentary way. She didn't hold back. She didn't even think twice about holding back. She threw the full complimentary force of her observation out there. I saw my friend hold his head up proudly then melt visibly from a formal business façade to a warm, approachable man. In making him feel good about himself, she repaid the debt of his time for her program and, in the bargain, made a new friend for life. She also broke down artificial emotional barriers that would have, otherwise, kept her at arm's length. When the two parted ways, a couple of hours later, they shared a quick, friendly hug.

Engagement

Always use the full impact of your eyes and smile. In the hustle and bustle of a world that never stops, this tip works more powerfully now than ever. Taking the time to look someone in the eyes and connect for a moment can reach deep down to the soul of a person. It's almost as rare as calling customer service and having an actual person answer the phone rather than an automated voice. We're losing too much human contact in today's society. That's why these techniques, long touted by the women of the South, will high-heel kick you to the top of someone's favorite-persons list. Look into his eyes for a deep connection and smile warmly. The eyes will draw him to you, and the smile will wrap him in gracious hospitality. It is an irresistible feeling in a world that is often far too cold.

Sparkle

Use all the aforementioned techniques to create an aura from the inside out that gives you a twinkle in the eye and a glitter that surrounds you. People are always drawn to sparkly things. When you need an extra boost, just whisper to yourself, "Sparkle, sparkle, sparkle." It lifts your spirits and enhances your twinkle immediately.

FLIRT ALERT:

Accumulate knowledge. You never know what you'll need to know.

THE FLIRTER BECOMES THE FLIRTEE

It's extremely rare for someone to flirt with me first. It's hard to beat me to the punch on the first wink. It happened, though, one day when I was lunching with my mother, and the experience strongly reminded me why social flirting works so well: because it feels good. It makes you feel so incredible that you do things you wouldn't have done otherwise.

Mama and I had just been seated and were looking over the menu when a handsome waiter came over. In beautifully accented English (he was from Cuba) he asked for our drink order, but before we could answer, he looked at me and blurted out, "You are gorgeous! You are most beautiful woman possible." (Beauty, of course, lies in the eye of the accomplished flirt.)

"Thank you," I replied, quite stunned by the sudden outburst.

"No, this I mean." He put his hand to his chest. "You take breath from me."

Well, that was just the beginning. He went on and on. Mama, of course, doesn't like to be left out from any boasting and praising going on, so she smiled up at him flirtatiously and said, "That's my baby."

He caught his cue perfectly. "Aw. Now, I see where such great beauty comes." He threw his hand toward her with flourish. "You give beauty and charm to her."

She giggled girlishly and replied, "Oh, you are so sweet."

Let me tell you—it was working. His tip was getting bigger by the moment. Each time he came to the table, he flattered, finessed, and flirtatiously finagled. When he brought the check, he had discounted my entrée. As he laid the check down, he said with a sweet sigh, "You make my day. Thank you. One day if I marry beautiful woman like you, I will be very happy man."

By the time that Romeo left the table, Mama and I both

were digging deep into our purses to pull out every dollar we had. That's the first time in my life that I ever left a tip bigger than the bill!

That, quite simply, is the power of social flirting.

BASIC COMMON COURTESIES

Flirting in its purest form is far removed from the sexy initiative that leads to romance and then to seduction. Take all the frills, boas, and sensuous lingerie away and you have a social skill that is unparalleled. Social flirting moves mountains and reduces an ocean of difference between folks to a mere trickle. It makes life more pleasant and business more enjoyable.

Approachable

Use direct eye contact and a welcoming smile to encourage folks to mosey over and meet you. The most important accessory to wear every day is a smile. Keep the corners of your mouth turned up as you walk through the mall, sit in a lecture, or are stalled in traffic. It becomes habit—a pleasant one that makes others want to know you better. Nothing is grimmer and more unappealing than someone whose mouth is turned down so often that it becomes permanent. Avoiding eye contact in a room or a meeting tells others that you do not want to be bothered. Simply put, look at people and smile. You'll soon find yourself making new friends of folks who used to be strangers in airports, restaurants, stores, and your own office building.

Warm

Just because it's business or a formal occasion doesn't mean you have to be icy or aloof. Speak in a tone that is rich in warmth, and use the person's name as much as possible.

Firm Handshake

Touching is crucial to truly terrific social flirting. By shaking a person's hand solidly, you're taking the time to hand off a portion of your energy and enthusiasm. I met a journalism legend who had inspired me during my days in journalism school. She shook my hand—a longtime admirer—by giving me only the tips of three fingers. It shattered my reverence for her. In essence, she was saying that I wasn't worthy of a decent handshake. To create social intimacy, it is also appropriate to lightly touch a sleeve or hand while in conversation. Southerners believe that the first handshake you receive from a person is indicative of his quality. Make it strong, firm, and assured.

Light Embrace

Southerners hug a lot. That's a wide-open secret to the success of our social flirting. People have an innate need to be hugged. If conversation is handled appropriately and a bonding occurs, we hug after knowing someone for a few hours. Just do it lightly and don't use the full-body press. Lean over from your space over to hug, and don't press your breasts against the person. I had dinner one night with a friend from South Carolina, along with her New York agent, his wife, and their two pre-teen daughters. I had spent only a couple of hours with them but when we parted in the parking lot, we all hugged. It was a lovely coming together and a fitting end to a warm and a delightful evening. It was especially beautiful to see the South embrace the North like that!

Smart Conversation

Besides being well-versed on different subjects, always be ready with an entertaining, brief story. Southerners excel in storytelling, particularly funny ones in which the storyteller takes the brunt of the joke. Folks like to be entertained and they gravitate to those who entertain with a good story. Develop this art form, even if you must work it out on paper or practice it in front of the mirror. (I'll elaborate on the technique of flirtatious storytelling in the next section.)

Wink

A jolly reminder of goodwill. It helps keep levity in situations, and that's always good. Trouble starts when things get too serious. I've winked across the table in board meetings as well to punctuate a statement or a story. Winks work equally well in boardrooms and bedrooms. Just in different ways.

Professional "Matchmaking"

The best incarnation of social flirting is making connections between people. Learn to love introducing people who should be doing business together. It is rare to find a greater pleasure than that of putting friends and acquaintances together who can make money and produce successful results. It's a game to many Southern women. Men, Southern or not, are not good at this. If they were, they would be much more successful. Southern women, though, will meet a new person at a business event and, after a lively conversation, will think of an important introduction that should be made. Reward always comes back to the matchmaker in the form of grateful friends.

Gifts of Gratitude

Never take without giving. The number one rule of Southern womanhood is handwritten thank-you notes. Don't stop there. Send a small gift (or large one if the favor is big), a gift certificate to a favorite restaurant or spa and, if it's a woman, a bouquet of flowers. Professional women love to see those big flowers being toted into their offices. Nothing is ruder than to take of a person's time and expertise and then fail to say thank you. Joanne, from a small town in Pennsylvania, had done a generous favor. I searched for just the right gift of appreciation and found it in a unique purse, hand decorated with beads and buttons. She loved it, and because it was so different, she always thought of her Southern friend when she used it. It also became a chat maker (more about that later) and brought her many new acquaintances. "This purse," she said, "has many admirers and now I know people I would never have known without it." She explained that she had been going to a church for several years—she even sang in the choir each Sunday—but had not met a lot of people. When she carried the purse, though, strangers began to gently morph into friends after many people initiated conversations over the unique purse.

Saying Thank You

A key aspect of social flirting is taking the time to express gratitude. By letting others know that you appreciate them or their efforts and skills, you make emotional deposits into their bank of goodwill. If an airport ticket agent is trying to find you another flight after the cancellation of one, say, "I really appreciate your efforts. Thank you for working so hard for me." She'll work harder and will stop at nothing to find you another flight. Very often, I say, at the conclusion of a business-related phone call or e-mail, "I appreciate you." And I do. And those people appreciate hearing that they're appreciated. Too often in today's self-centered world, people do not hear those mighty words, "Thank You."

Social flirting is charming and effective. When in doubt as to what is appropriate in a business environment, just do what is courteous and deeply thoughtful. You can't go wrong.

STORIES TOLD FROM VOICES BOLD

A good storyteller holds magic in the delicate palm of her hand. It's like holding stardust that you can toss over a crowd and instantly make it captivated and mesmerized. It is the atomic weapon of an industrial-strength flirt. It is possible to be an excellent storyteller without being a good flirt. *It is not possible, however, to be an excellent flirt without being a decent storyteller.* In *1001 Arabian Nights*, Shahrazad held the king captivated and, in the bargain, spared her life and won his heart with her storytelling ways. In all forms of flirting—social, courtship, and seductive—the ability to tell interesting stories is a chief component.

It's hard to top a Southern storyteller. The literary world would be much poorer without the musings of Southern writers, including two women who headed the American Library Association list for most significant books of the twentieth century: Alabama's Harper Lee was number one with the Pulitzer Prize–winning *To Kill a Mockingbird*, followed by Georgia's Margaret Mitchell, who penned *Gone With the Wind*, another Pulitzer Prize winner. Pop culture, too, would suffer severely without the steady stream of contributions from Southern novelists. Why? Because superb storytelling is practiced, preached, and taught in the South from living rooms to front porches to classrooms to pulpits.

I attended a book conference outside of the South where I was introduced to a local resident. When he discovered where I was from, the man laughed and said, "You're from the South? I didn't know that people in the South actually read!"

Strengthened by the South's great literary heritage, I looked him squarely in the eye and replied, "Sir, not only do we read but most of the time, we *write* what the rest of the world reads!"

Enormous population and economic growth is now overtaking the South but for two previous centuries, it was largely rural. With little else to do on Saturday nights and Sunday afternoons, folks visited and tried to do outdo each other by creating yarns and fables, in addition to tossing in well-executed, often embellished true stories. Amusement and entertainment were passed around kitchen tables in the South as often as plates of steaming hot biscuits. To this day, the heart of a Southern home lies in the kitchen, where food and well-told stories, both hallmarks of Southern life, are shared. Here are the techniques that will turn anyone into a captivating storyteller.

ELEMENTS OF STORYTELLING

To tell a good story, you must first be able to recognize one. Someone once asked famed Georgia writer Flannery O'Connor why Southerners wrote so much about freaks. "Because," she answered flatly, "we are still able to recognize them." The same goes for a story. It doesn't have to be a huge story about a major event like a robbery or fire in order to keep listeners spellbound. Children matching wits with each other, a flight that's almost missed, car keys misplaced but found in the fridge, or a chance encounter with an oddball—the best storytellers find entertaining drama in ordinary events and common occurrences.

The Beginning

Develop a good opening line such as "Wait till you hear this!" The tone of the story is set by the tone of your voice—it should be enthusiastic—used for this opening line. Southerners frequently begin our stories with, "You're not going to believe this!" From beginning to end, treat the story as a mini-theatrical event, and your audience will respond.

Romantic Language

The best Southern storytellers intersperse a story with romantic, lyrical words not often used today. Shakespeare and the King James Version of the Bible are excellent resources for romantic language. Those powerful words ring pleasingly and seductively in the listener's ears. Here are some examples:

Ponder rather than think
Mirth rather than laughter
Gaily rather than happily
Rising up rather than got up
I shall never forget rather than I will never forget
Shan't rather than won't
Pontificated rather than said
Bodacious rather than grand
Distraught rather than upset
Banter rather than chat
Nary rather than none
Miss Priss rather than Mary
Prance rather than walk

Imagination

No story ever suffered at the hands of a good embellisher. Remember when we were children, unrestrained by reality, and we told great stories the way we saw them in our minds? Do that now. Without fabricating, dress the stories up with your imagination. Describe mountains that are large, casting the earth in their shadows; the special shade of pink that streaks gently and slightly across the sky before sundown; the booming sound of an authoritative voice and the heaviness of footsteps falling against a wood floor or a dog that speaks clearly in a language you understand perfectly. See a story as it should be, not necessarily as it is.

One day my Mama was telling a story about my brother. When she finished, he rolled his eyes and said, "Now, as long as that took her to tell (about ten or twelve minutes), it all happened in about two minutes." I knew that was the truth. No one embellishes a story better than my Mama and, for the most part, no one tells a better story than she does.

Plenty of Adjectives and Adverbs

Beautify a story with descriptive words. Most people tell straightforward stories that are bland. Decorating your stories with sparkly words is akin to adding a magnificent bow to a package.

I was going over samples of fabric and wallpaper with Rudy, an interior designer I always work with, when I spied the perfect combination. "This is it!" I announced triumphantly. "This will be so cute!"

Rudy threw his shoulders back, folded his arms, cast his eyes to the ceiling, and declared with a trembling pout, "I don't do cute." He paused for a moment to stick out his lower lip and then continued. "I do spectacular, fabulous, magnificent, pretty, gorgeous, stunning, handsome, breathtaking, sensational, beautiful, to-die-for-glorious, wonderful, and I have, on occasion, done bodacious. But never, under any circumstances, have *I* done *cute*."

See, now that's the kind of adjective use I'm talking about.

Colorful Imagery

Conjure up images for the listeners. Put them there with you. In vivid language, describe the red leather booths, the heat of the humid summer afternoon, the lemon-yellow dress decorated with a meringue-colored collar, the wave crashing thunderously against the shore. When you tell a story, others are creating the imagery in their minds. Give them plenty to work with.

Sentence Mixing and Matching

Combine short, strong sentences with long, lyrical ones. Use a dramatic pause after the short ones then breeze into the longer, floral ones. This variety will keep the listener enthralled.

> *And there he stood. (Pause) Anger drifting quietly across his face like the silent, dark clouds that precede a deadly tornado on an unsuspecting spring afternoon. (Pause) It was quite a sight to behold.*

Voice Tone

When the words are lyrical, use a melodic sound, with your voice rising and falling in a rolling cadence. Switch tones to fit specific portions of the story: disbelief, sweetness, humor, puzzlement, etc. Above all, put your full heart behind each word.

Sidebars

Southern women are unbeatable at adding commentary to our stories whenever possible. Sidebars are little vignettes that don't quite fit into the telling of the main story yet add interest and information. In the South, sidebars inevitably include who's kin to whom, and other popular sidebars include what food was served, who looked particularly lovely that day, who didn't, and more. Be creative.

Details

Whatever you do, don't tell a story like a man does. *Boring*. Never bother to ask a man questions about an incident after he has just given the major pieces of information. He has told you all he knows and all he cared to find out. While most men suffer at the art of storytelling, they are captivated by women who are gifted at it. Cover the basics—what, when, how, who and why, then add decorative flourishes. Entertain as well as inform.

Suspense

Build it. Don't give away your ending. I know storytellers who would prefer to slit their own throats rather than unveil a story's ending before the perfect time. Keep 'em guessing until the end.

Drama

Southern women are dramatic. Every event is a production, especially stories. Hair isn't the only thing we like big. We like our stories grand, infusing them with overwrought drama in the form of tone, gestures, and expressions. Use all the props it takes to fittingly tell the story right.

Analogies

Use analogies that are indicative of your personal style and culture. Spend some time developing five or six and keep them in your storytelling repertoire. This adds flavor to your personality. It is especially endearing when you hearken back to something that has a connection to a time gone by. We have created our own in my family. My grandmother grew up near a family named Dewberry. From all accounts, the Dewberrys never cleaned their house and littered their yards with trash, old cars, sofas with springs poking through the fabric, and other such unsightly clutter. As a result, my Mama is known to often say when she needs to clean, "The house looks like the Dewberrys live here!" What an image that always concocts whenever I hear her say it.

Look for a way to always be interesting in conversation and storytelling even if it isn't with an analogy. When I was barely in my teens, I was visiting a great-aunt who lived in a rambling Victorian house with a wraparound porch. Several female relatives were enjoying the autumn afternoon, sitting in rocking chairs and watching as people strolled by on the sidewalks. When one of the town's best-looking flirts pranced by in a pretty dress and high heels, one of the ladies stopped her rocker and said, "I'd like to buy her for what she's worth and sell her for what she *thinks* she's worth."

"That'd be good," another responded. "You could make yourself a millionaire."

It was a colorful way of saying that she thought more of herself than, in their opinions, she had any right to.

Humor

Southern storytellers often employ self-effacing humor, which is enormously appealing to their audience. Tell the story about your smeared mascara, disheveled outfit, or self-inflicted stupidity or the day you ran into your husband's ex-girlfriend when she looked stunning and you looked "like a poor excuse for the reason he broke up with her."

Strong Delivery

When you tell a story, command attention. Your confidence will continue to grow as you tell more and more stories and receive positive feedback. People enjoy hearing stories from a person who enjoys telling them. So be lively, self-assured, and engaging. But remember to be courteous and not hog all the attention and time in a conversation. When you have dinner with friends, plan on telling one to two good stories during the course of the evening.

Morals and Parables

Not all stories are funny. Some are thought-provoking and can affect the listener in a profound way. I spew forward with these kinds of stories—lessons learned and philosophies formed—constantly, probably to the distress of my friends, though some tend to like the wisdom that springs forth. Flirtation should always be girded with substance. Smart, thought-provoking stories do that. Truly terrific storytellers see both the wit *and* the wisdom of life, and they share that. Train yourself to see lessons in situations that can be turned to anecdotes. Once this becomes a habit, it will become a natural part of your thinking process. You'll be standing in a grocery store line, overhear an exchange between a mother and a child, and suddenly have a new story to share. The bottom line is: People like to be entertained, to be transcended momentarily from their world into another. Good stories of all kinds do just that.

The Last Word

Use powerful words to conclude the story. Often, it's just one strong sentence delivered dramatically with a punchy flourish. In the South, our women over-dramatize. Even the simplest story—one about an afternoon whiled away on the phone—can be finished memorably with something like, "And there, my friend, you have it. The woeful tale of a sadly wasted afternoon."

FLIRT ALERT:

Never let facts get in the way of a good story!
Southerners certainly don't.

Practice storytelling in the written word as well as spoken. My dear friend Virgie is a wonderful Mississippi belle. To me, she is the doyenne of Southern womanhood perfection. Like most Mississippians, she tells a compelling story in person and on paper. I asked permission to share the following excerpt from a personal letter to me, and she responded, "Absolutely. We must do all we can to help other women become enlightened to the Southern way of doing things! We have to hoist that flag up and hold it high. It's not fair for us to know these things and not share them."

Virgie was describing the first time she discovered flirting—at seven years old, when boy on whom she had a crush had unintentionally caused her to fall from the playground swing when he pushed the swing too hard and too high. She and her little brother, Sammy, had then fled the playground and taken off for her grandmother's.

"We never went home from playing. It was always to Granny's for afternoon treats and Granny coddling. I went down the street, wiping a tear or two off and looking behind me, hoping that somehow my love would be following me. He was not.

At Granny's, of course, as soon as she saw my dirty face with tear tracks on it, she grabbed me and more tears flowed. Sammy told her what happened. 'That Ladnier boy tried to kill Virgie

Ann on the swings but I stopped him.' Granny, of course, assessed the situation immediately as I had barely mentioned him to her once. She sent Sammy out in the backyard, past the fences that separated the lawn, past the fence that led into her English garden, into the back area where the chicken house, goat shed, the fig trees, and the garden grew. She knew he would become engaged in a million little-boy investigations and we would be good for an hour. Of course, he had a fistful of cookies with him.

We sat down on the front porch with a glass of iced sugar tea and some little egg salad finger sandwiches on a plate, our afternoon tea party. Immediately, she said, 'That boy was flirting with you.' That was not the first time I had heard the words, but that was the first time it was identified to a behavior that I was involved in."

Get the picture? I thought so. Southerners believe that the only thing that beats a good story is a great story that can be told and retold, especially in social flirting situations. Storytelling brings people together and creates connections. There is a special bonding in the entertainment of storytelling because others don't have to express opinion or contribute commentary. They can relax, listen, and enjoy. Socially, nothing is more seductive. Look at all the money that is spent annually on entertainment. *Remember: You cannot be a good flirt without being a good storyteller.* It's impossible. With it, though, you can charm the world.

Social flirting is one of the great assets that can be developed throughout life. By following the basics at the beginning of this chapter and learning to be a terrific storyteller, no one will be able to outcharm you!

CHAPTER FOUR

GOODWILL COMES TO
THOSE WHO WINK

At a major library-books show in Dallas, I was appearing in my publisher's booth when a middle-aged man and young lady approached. He was a fast talker who was on a specific mission: He was trying to build up business for his restaurant. Smartly, he knew that the thousands who were attending the event would need a place for dinner that evening, so he and one of his employees were working the show, handing out coupons for free appetizers and singing the praises of the food and ambiance. He was a little too aggressive for me but, as is the way of most Southerners, I tolerated it and treated him with consideration, though his pushiness was putting a strain on my manners.

Mr. Fast Talker and I were tolerating each other just fine when my New York City friend Virginia came charging back to the booth from an errand. *Charging* is the perfect word to describe the fast-paced gait of this no-nonsense woman. She is prompt, professional, and efficient. As a publisher's rep, she was working the event like a Texas tornado. Instantly, she cast a look of doubt in the direction of Mr. Fast Talker and company. Then, as a courteous, well-bred Southerner, I made the introductions. He offered his hand, and she reluctantly took it for a quick handshake while I explained, "He owns a restaurant in town."

"What are you doing for dinner tonight?" he asked cordially, preparing to launch into his sales bit.

She snatched her hand back as if a snake had bitten her, grabbed a nearby director's chair, and slammed it down directly between them. Her eyes narrowed. Then, as her cheeks burned to crimson red with suspicion, she asked bluntly, "*What do you want?*"

He physically withdrew a bit while I started laughing at the extremeness of her reaction. I looked over at him and winked. "Don't be offended," I advised. "She's Long Island born and bred. She just sees the world a bit differently than Southerners."

"You're from Long Island?" he asked.

She pinched her lips together and glared. "Yeah. Whatta 'bout it?"

"Me, too! Where did you go to high school?"

She opened the door ever so slightly in her brick wall and used one blue eye to peep out cautiously. Still skeptical, she tersely answered his questions. Now that's the big difference between the North and the South. Had someone told me that he grew up near me, I would have run around the table that was separating us and hugged his neck. Before it was over, we would have found out exactly how we were kin because surely we would have relatives in common somewhere. But Long Island, apparently, doesn't work that way. I watched all this with amusement. Especially when the man tried to take advantage of their common ground and close the deal.

FLIRT ALERT:

One wink and a man doesn't stop to think.

"So, since we're both from Long Island, you'll come to dinner tonight at my restaurant?" he asked.

Virginia frowned. "We already have reservations elsewhere. I'm not inclined to change them."

I stepped forward. "But we're willing to consider a deal." Accomplished social flirters enjoy getting something for nothing more than a smile and a wink. "What would you give us if we cancel those reservations and come to your place instead?" I smiled flirtatiously and winked playfully. *Social flirters always look for ways to make a situation more advantageous.* Since the proposition is lighthearted and witty, the sweet victim is normally game for offering favors, and I am always game for accepting them. Virginia's mouth dropped open but she stayed silent.

"I'm giving you this coupon for a free appetizer," he replied.

"Yeah but we want more. After all, we already have a reservation at a highly touted restaurant, and we'll have to go to the trouble to cancel that. Plus, your restaurant is an unknown commodity to us." I spread my hands and shrugged. "No one has recommended it like the other one." I smiled and fluttered my eyelashes.

He chuckled. "Okay. I'll give you both free dessert."

Virginia's eyes widened. "That's very nice," I replied in the sweetest tone. "And we'll certainly take that. But I was also thinking that we should get a buy-one-entrée, get-one-free."

Virginia's eyes almost popped out. So did his. Then Virginia started to laugh. "This is my girl," she told him, slinging her head in my direction. "I count on her to do all our negotiation. She's got that Southern charm going, you know."

He played hard to get for a while, but I persisted, socially flirting to the point that the poor man was beat up. Finally, he waved the white flag. "Okay, okay, okay. You're driving a hard bargain on a poor business man, even though you're on a company expense account. It's not even money out of your own pocket. But I'll do it. I'll make a reservation for you at seven-fifteen."

"We're not promising," the cynic said, waving a nail-bitten finger at him. "But we'll see."

She was a harder sell than he was, but I convinced her, albeit reluctantly, that we should go for the fun of it. "Besides," I promised, "If we get there and it isn't an elegant restaurant, we'll go to the other one we were planning to go to."

All the way over in the cab, she fussed and worried. I knew she was agitated because she clutched her purse to her chest and appeared to be in battle mode. "I'm telling you that he probably forgot us the moment he left. He's just a fast talker. We're going to get there and not even have a reservation."

"I doubt it," I replied.

We entered the door of the beautifully appointed, elegant restaurant, and the maitre d' greeted us. "May I help you, ladies?"

"Yes. We have a reservation," I said.

He grinned broadly. "You must be Virginia and Ronda! I have you down for seven-fifteen."

Virginia made absolutely no effort to hide her astonishment. Her mouth dropped, her eyes widened, and then, shaking her head in amazement, she looked at me. I smiled triumphantly.

"You're early and the table isn't ready yet. Would you mind waiting in the bar?"

Off we went, Virginia dragging behind me, muttering with wonderment. Once seated, the waiter brought appetizers and drinks.

"We didn't order those," Virginia said bluntly.

The waiter smiled. "M'am, it's all on the house. Mr. Morgan said to tell you that he'll be in shortly to see you."

Virginia shook her head while amazement melted into amusement. "That's the most incredible thing I've ever seen. How do you do that?"

"It's called 'social flirting,' and you should practice it sometime," I said, teasing.

"And you," replied my publishing friend, "should write a book about it!"

FLIRT ALERT:

Play nice. Even if you aren't

The unfortunate aspect of social flirting in such a successful way is that it sets a high standard that folks like Virginia expect on a constant basis. Such was the case the next day when I decided I would go to the airport and try to get an earlier flight. I called the airline and was forewarned that there was virtually no chance of it happening since the flight was overbooked.

"You can do it," Virginia replied confidently. "Just do that Southern thing you do." I was reluctant to set myself up in what appeared to be a no-win situation. She persisted—this after spending an entire morning bragging about the restaurant adventure to everyone who came by the booth—so I had no choice. I headed to the airport where the counter agent said, "I'm sorry. There's no chance you're getting on that flight. We're overbooked and we have forty passengers in front of you for standby."

My spirits sank but I put forth my best social flirting effort. In addition to being friendly and smiling, I chatted away, telling her that I wanted to get home as soon as possible because I had to leave the next day on an extensive trip. We had a conversation about life in general and created an immediate bond. I complimented her lipstick, and we discussed how difficult it is to find the right shade. Then, as I prepared to head to the gate, I thanked her profusely ending with a "Thank you very much for your kindness" and a wink.

She smiled broadly. "Thank you for being so pleasant."

I called Virginia from my cell phone because she had instructed me to call in. "So?" she asked when she answered. I explained the situation and how it didn't look good.

My ardent admirer replied with complete confidence, "I'm not worried. Just keep doing that Southern thing you do and you'll be on the flight."

Knowing my reputation for social flirting was really on the line, I trudged forward. I went to the gate agent and made my appeal. Remember: *Flirting of any kind is about being real nice to the other person.*

"My goodness!" I said as I looked around at the passengers spilled to overflowing. "Y'all are really busy!"

"Yeah," he replied. "We've had a flight canceled due to high winds and now we're trying to get people to Atlanta to make connecting flights."

My spirits sank and I let it show on my face like a pitiful puppy. "Oh," I said meekly. "I guess that doesn't bode well for me getting on an earlier flight to Atlanta, does it?"

He sighed deeply. "Probably not, but let me look." About that time, the captain of the plane came over to check on something else, and he entered the conversation with us.

"Are you going to be able to put her on this flight?" the captain asked as the agent finished typing.

"Doesn't look like it. She's on the standby list but there're forty-three in front of her."

"Forty-three!" I exclaimed. "When I left the ticket counter, it was only forty. How did three more get in front of me?"

"Higher frequent-flyer status," he said, as though it pained him to tell me. I saw an opening.

I leaned over and whispered softly to him, "So, does that mean you can move people up on the list?" I winked conspiratorially. "You have that power?"

The captain started laughing. "Yeah, Joe, you have that power, don't you."

Joe shook his head comically and rolled his eyes. I moved in. "Oh please? It'll mean so much to me to get home and get a good night's sleep before I leave again tomorrow. Please use your power for me." I leaned closer and smiled playfully. "And, if you'll check, you'll see that I have twelve flights in the next ten days on your airline." I batted my eyelashes, also managing to look pitifully playful at the same time. "Please help me if you can. You're a wonderful man. I know you are. I can tell by looking at you." I winked teasingly. "And you have power."

He was melting. I turned a flirtatious face to the captain who threw up his hands and said, "Don't look at me. I just fly the plane. He's the one who has that authority."

I laughed. "Okay, Joe. You just do whatever you can and just know that I'll appreciate it from the deepest depths of my heart." I winked again while theatrically throwing my hand against my heart. In that one sentence, I did two important things: I called him by his name, which quickly assists in melting resistance; I also created drama when I talked about the "deepest depths of my heart." *Drama adds humor, and humor is the greatest ally of all.*

Joe shook his head and laughed. "I'm not making any promises. Go have a seat, and I'll see what I can do."

When my name was announced at the last minute as being added to the passenger's list, I gasped with delight and jumped up from my seat. I grabbed my bag and flew over to the counter. "Thank you! Thank you! Thank you!" I gushed to the red-faced agent. "I hope you have the best life possible." Forty or so glum-looking passengers were left behind as I took my place in line.

While edging slowly toward the gate, I dialed Virginia from my cell phone and shouted excitedly, "I'm on!"

She howled with laughter and screamed to others near by, "She's on!!!" I heard gales of laughter on the other end. "I knew you could do it! It's that Southern thing." Laughing, my

New York friend said, "I'm in total admiration. You Southern women are really something."

When I got on the plane, the captain was standing at the door. When he saw me, he, too, laughed. "So, you did make it! Somehow I had a feeling you would."

Why does social flirting work in situations like those two in Dallas?

Because people like to do things for people they like or folks who appeal to them because of soothing or amusing actions, particularly in today's environment when troubles and worry all too often abound. That's why the job doesn't always go to the best qualified. Sometimes it goes to the best liked. Social flirting is a salve for a society wounded too often by barbs, digs, and backstabbing. Quite simply, human nature is to move toward pleasure and away from pain or discomfort. *People are naturally drawn toward those who are uplifting with words, smiles, winks, and basic good humor.* Aren't you? If you have two phone calls to return and one is from someone who berates, grumbles, and argues while the other is from someone who is cheerful, complimentary and reasonable, which one will you call immediately? Which call will you dread and put off?

To Gain a Good Deal From Goodwill, Practice:

Fun bantering. Nothing puts someone in a good mood better than someone who is quick on the draw with observations, comments, and comebacks.

Playful wink. It's the perfect punctuation to a lighthearted request or negotiation.

Flattery. Everyone, particularly those in customer service positions, need a cheery word. Lay it on them with a lavish hand.

Smile. It's unbeatable in its ability to pull you in to others' goodwill.

Laugh. At yourself, at the situation, at the other person's comment. Laughter draws folks together.

Personable. Call a person by his first name, look him in the eye, shake his hand, find common issues to discuss.

Observe. Watch for the smallest details like I did when I seized upon the gate agent's name and quickly realized that he had the power to move me up on the list.

Positive thoughts. No matter how dire the situation seems, regardless of what science says is possible, you always have a chance. Always. Give it a shot. When you put positive energy into the universe, it dances right back in your hands. Just like chicks of a feather who flock together, the same happens with positive actions because like actions attract each other. Your goodwill toward someone else lures goodwill back to you.

Courteous manners. It's the old Golden Rule theory: Treat people like you would like to be treated and, more often than not, that's how you'll be treated. Unless it's just a real mean person, your kindness will be mirrored in the actions of others.

You don't always have to see a wink to know it's there. It's possible to make your voice wink over the phone. Just act as you would if you were face to face by smiling and winking. The other person will "hear" your wink and will respond accordingly. It works. Recently, I was having terrible problems with a higher-tech-than-I-am-smart cell phone. Customer support, and the store from which it had been bought, was clueless to what the problem was. Finally, the company put me in touch with their product expert, who turned out to be a single guy. He also turned out to be my "knight in shining armor," which I told him repeatedly and which he loved.

"Oh goodness." I sighed. "I don't know what I would have ever done without you! You're my hero. Honest."

Finally, I had to send him my cell phone, which takes and stores photos. He returned the phone, all fixed up and included complimentary accessories. I also discovered his photo in my phone with all of his phone numbers. He sent a handwritten note that read, "I'm only an easy call away if you need any help."

We never met personally but that California guy had felt the inducement of a wink through the phone line. It had traveled with full force from one coast to another to prove that goodwill comes to those who wink, either in person or by long distance.

A wink is the perfect punctuation to a flirtatious remark, a teasing comment, or a compliment. It signals approval, friendship, and warmth. It can bring the mightiest men to their knees and turn a unfriendly woman into a friend. Amazing how something so small can have such big power.

CHAPTER FIVE

CHARMNACITY

Have you ever noticed that when people talk or write about a woman of undeniable Southern upbringing, the one word of description inevitably used is *charming*? People are both fascinated and seduced by charm. Politicians are elected by charm more than by issues. Stars become superstars based as much on charm as talent, and athletes who are charming earn millions in endorsement contracts as opposed to their noncharming teammates who have to work harder on the field to have any name recognition.

Charm, quite simply, is the name of the game. Especially in social flirting. Southern women add an extra component to charm. We strengthen the prettiness of it with iron will and tough-as-acrylic-nails tenacity. Long called steel magnolias, Southern women prove it's true by employing charmnacity, a descriptive blending of the words *charm* and *tenacity*. When sweetness and cajolery don't work, we pull off the white gloves and the battle begins.

"My mother was a pretty Southern belle who always said that she did her part for the unity of our nation and married a Yankee," one New York friend explained. "There was never any doubt who ran our family. That delicate, whimsical Southern belle had that no-nonsense Yankee wrapped fetchingly around her little finger. Normally, she got her way by spoiling him and babying him. But, on the rare occasion that didn't work, her toughness put the toughness of my father to shame!"

Southern women are artisans at employing tenacious charm that wears down resistance and turns previously avowed foes into devoted followers and impossible situations into favorable ones. While the first image often conjured up when the subject of Southern women arises is that of lovely, feminine women with honeyed drawls who ooze charm, you can ask anyone who has dealt with a Southern woman at length, and he will explain that the charm masks an approach to life that is unrivaled in its toughness and determination. Simply put, we know that *any situation can be conquered through charm and tenacity.* Sometimes one does not work without the other but used together and used constantly, it is an undefeatable combination

FLIRT ALERT:

All women may be created equal, but some are unequal in the creation they become.

There is a code, both spoken and unspoken, among Southern women that calls for attention to appearance. It is an offshoot of that enormous pride that haunted us long before Sherman took his vile vengeance. We can priss, prance, flutter, and flounce with the best and for those highly-envied skills, we make no apology. On the other side of the glossy magnolia leaf, we revel in camaraderie with friends as well as with those we scarcely know, scatter compassion like rose petals blowing in the gentle summer breeze, and tote casseroles in baskets to those who are in need of a gesture of kindness. Yes, there is a certain amount of light-spirited frivolity to the women of the South, but there is a greater amount of substance. For friends, acquaintances, and strangers in need, a woman raised by these standards, preached by mothers from the Carolinas to Texas, will be there in two shakes of a nail polish bottle. While we fight strongest for our families and ourselves, we also love a good fight for the sake of all womanhood, as in the case of my friend Jenny, who was all in a huff about that feminist from God-knows-where-but-certainly-not-the-South, who was trying to force a Southern country club to admit women by yakking about it on television.

"What kind of woman draws attention to herself in such an unseemly fashion?" asked one of the best practitioners of charmnacity that I have ever known.

I couldn't answer that. That kind of woman is alien to the kind of smoothly strategic women I know.

"Well, I'll just tell you this—if we Southern women had ever wanted to be members of such a place, we'd be members!" she continued while I nodded in agreement. "And *we* would have done it the *right* way. We wouldn't have gone on national television and bullied. It's so unladylike." She shuddered delicately. "There's a gentler way of getting one's way, as we Southern women know." She dusted her hands together. "We'd've just gone right over there and charmed them and that would have been that. I've never seen a man yet who could say no to me after eating my peach cobbler, a recipe that, by the way, comes from my great-grandmother of the Gulfport Davises. Besides, who cares if men have their own fraternizing clubs? They need to have somewhere to go while we go shopping. Then, as I see it, the score is all even. Neither side can complain."

Jenny, former Kudzu Queen, is right. Southern women know that charm mixed with tenacity will get a woman anything that her little ol' heart desires. Apparently, the little ol' hearts of Deep Dixie had never desired a membership in the male club.

"Why is it necessary for a woman to belong to an elite social club when there are so many other issues of importance facing women?" I mused thoughtfully. She slapped her hand down on the table, causing her grandmother's fine china teacups to jiggle, and sloshing tea on her antique walnut table.

"My point exactly! For instance, a bank where my husband, Edgar, and I have kept most of our money on deposit for the past few years, has no women in senior management or on their board of directors! I have been grousing about it for a couple of years, but when they had the audacity to run an ad campaign showing all these men who are *in charge*, I dashed right down to the bank and closed my account. I moved it over to another one where women are appreciated and properly promoted within their ranks. Of course, they paid no attention to me so I told Edgar that he'd best get down there and move all of his money, too, and if he didn't, I could promise that he would, in fact, soon be moving fifty percent of it when I divorced him!" She chortled delightedly, and I asked what happened.

"Honey, need you ask? Of course, he moved it immediately." She winked. "He told the bank president that women not only have a great deal of earning power, we also have a lot of *churning* power. We know how to keep a man's stomach churning until he does what we want! I was so proud of him for being such a good boy that I pulled out a naughty red teddy that night and showed him proper how much I appreciated him moving that mountain of money!"

Southern divas rally together for the good of womanhood and recognize the importance of choosing battles wisely. As Jenny proved, we definitely know how to practice the fine art of managing money *and* man!

GROW YOUR KUDZU NETWORK

Charmnacity is a key method used in social flirting. It is what inspires Southern women to host countless soirees and to attend every possible luncheon, tea, or civic gathering. This persistent approach to socializing creates a network of contacts that grows as quickly as kudzu in the summer heat of a vacant pasture. Kudzu is an insidious plant that scientists brought from Japan in the 1800s to stop the erosion that was plaguing the South. It is a monster and its growth cannot be stopped. It now covers over a million acres of Southern soil.

My friends Myra, Chantel, and Sharon have address books that are nothing short of encyclopedic; and having been the repeated recipient of their largesse, I know well how generous they are with sharing those contacts. From them, I have learned the importance and joy of matching acquaintances so they can do business together. It's quite simply a law of the universe—put goodwill out and it will multiply back to you like grits in a pot of boiling water. Think good of the world and good will be drawn back to you. It's a mental process that you control, and it also controls how others feel toward you. *Charmnacity begins with open friendliness and a genuine desire to help others.* Smart women look for opportunities to build their networks by helping others.

A young woman, about to graduate from college, appealed to me for assistance. She was a complete stranger, but her approach was so humble and earnest that I felt compelled to help her. She wanted to work in an arena of the entertainment industry where I have particularly strong contacts. I called a friend of mine who runs a major facility and asked if he would allow her to volunteer for a huge, upcoming event. He agreed. It was a good deal because she was going to pay all of her expenses, including airfare, and she was going to work for free. My friend passed the request to his director of public relations with the appropriate instructions. To make a long story short, the publicist, a young woman, handled everything very poorly, and in the end she turned down the college student, saying she had "way too many volunteers." (Is it possible, I've wondered ever since, to have too much free help?) This is an example of what not to do in life, especially when it comes to helping a friend of your boss's. But more than that, the publicist missed out on an opportunity to earn goodwill that would boomerang back into her life by doing good for someone else. She also nipped her kudzu network in the bud, because she lost me as well as another person as a contact.

I took full advantage of my kudzu network when I decided to launch a syndicated newspaper column about the South as seen through the eyes of its women. First, I visited former bosses and mentors from my days as a sportswriter and asked for guidance. I followed all their advice, including the strong suggestion that I syndicate the column myself, which meant I would have to do all the selling.

FLIRT ALERT:

No one will ever sell you better than you sell yourself. To be truly successful, go out and do your own selling because no one—except your mama—will ever believe more in you than you do.

Then I began calling up friends in the media, many who were either decision makers for their newspapers and/or knew other decision makers. Using this approach, I not only met but doubled my goal of subscribing newspapers in half the time I had set. I also didn't hesitate to call other non-newspaper friends and ask for introductions, such as in the case of my friend Charlie.

"Hey, do you have any poker-playing buddies who are in the newspaper business?" I asked, knowing how tight these fraternities are.

"As a matter of fact," he began, going on to tell me of a

good friend who owns a newspaper. That lead turned into the second subscriber for the column, with the publisher calling on other media buddies to consider carrying it as well. I learned that I sold my column to newspapers quicker if I could meet the decision makers face to face. I used all the best techniques of social flirting for professional situations including being charmnacious. I made it clear that I was passionate about what I was selling and, most important, presented reasons why my column would be a winner for their readers. Only twice have I been able to sell it without meeting the editor or publisher, and both of those times, I was introduced to those buyers through mutual acquaintances or friends.

FLIRT ALERT:

Sex sells. Anyone who disputes that doesn't have enough sex appeal to sell or give away. The way you package and present yourself goes a long way in making the sale.

CHARMNACITY NECESSITIES

Persistence

Today's no could turn quickly into tomorrow's yes. Situations and factors change quickly. Corporations merge; philosophies change, strategies are revamped, and there are constant shifts in managements and duties—and individual moods and desires. It is essential to remember that some triumphs take a lot of side roads and detours before victory is claimed. Don't give up.

Don't Take It Personally

Many decisions are made based on subjective opinion, not hard facts. Someone else might decide differently. I once got a job when the top boss voted against hiring me but left the decision to his second-in-charge, who gave me a chance. After I won several awards and increased the company's revenue stream, the top boss admitted his reservation about my hiring and how wrong he had been. I didn't mind hearing this—I was grateful for his candor and delighted to have proved his initial judgment wrong.

Don't Take It Lying Down

One yes will wipe out a thousand no's. Every time you are told no, just remember that it has taken you one step closer to the right yes. The doors that close aren't the ones that should open. Just keeping trying until the right door opens. Life's a numbers game. Whether you're looking for a job or a husband or playing the lottery, the more you play, the better your chances are.

Charms First, Arms Last

Don't get up in arms quickly and cause a disturbance. Squeeze every little bit out of your charm before you choose battle. And, if you do have to do battle, do it in a clever, charming way. Jenny used her feminine wiles by first addressing the issue with the bank, then she quickly moved to use her influence with her husband. A wise woman always ensures she has a strong voice with her husband by not nagging unnecessarily. She speaks clearly and with conviction when it is needed so that he heeds her requests. Nagging erodes a woman's influence. Then, like Jenny, he is rewarded in a very womanly way.

NEVER Accept Defeat

Even if you keep losing at the same situation, never give voice to the possibility of quitting. Don't say, "I give up" or "I can't do it." Say instead, "I am going to figure this out," "I am not giving up," "I'm going to regroup and come back." Your subconscious and your inner spirit know only what you tell them. So if you invite the thought of failure in or accept that you can be beaten, you have stepped into dangerous territory that could be littered with land mines in future battles for success.

This last point is the most critical in the art of charmnacity and probably the most important words in this book. You have to be very careful with the words you speak. With typical Southern superstition, Mama always said, "Be careful what you say. You'll speak it into existence." That's true for both good and bad. *Words take thoughts closer to action and, therefore, to reality.*

My best friend, Debbie, gave me a wonderful gift: a state-of-the-art personal organizer. In addition to a calendar and address book, that PDA can do everything from playing movies to surfing the Internet to downloading e-mail to taking photos. I set about learning all the electronics, and six weeks later, I still couldn't connect to the Internet or receive e-mail. I was frustrated and using a lot of valuable time, taking me away from business that would have generated income. Several people suggested that I should give up and stop spending so much time and energy on it. But I couldn't do that because, in the long run, quitting would have cost me much more than the bit of revenue I lost while learning the complexities of that mini computer.

Had I given up, I would have been opening the door to let future defeat in; to give myself permission to quit when something was too hard. I would have planted in my mind the seed of there-are-things-I-simply-can't-do. That seed, over time, would have grown to full term and, eventually, delivered more failure. So I stuck with it until I prevailed, through phone charm and tenacity. The use of charmnacity hooked me up with the company's top expert, who became *my* personal guide to the product. It took a few hours of coast-to-coast long-distance instruction, but, in the end, it finally worked flawlessly. In addition, a single guy and a single gal became cozy friends—as friends, we now talk weekly, proving again the effectiveness of charmnacity and social flirting.

CHAPTER SIX

RETURN ON ASSETS:
THE BUSINESS OF FLIRTING

Contrary to some opinions, social flirting is not out of place in the workplace or a professional environment, such as an office party or social gathering. As a sportswriter, I often found it was my most effective weapon. I got athletes who refused to even look at male sportswriters, to give me headline-making, career-boosting scoops. Nothing was inappropriate, nor did I ever step over the line. I merely used my ability as a smart woman who is able to engage others with conversation, courtesy, and charm and then succeeds in standing out in a crowd.

Just use all the assets you have—clever mind, big smile, twinkling eyes, lovely hands—to make your mark in business. By enhancing your work relationships with thoughtfulness, courtesy, and generosity, you will get attention and respect of female colleagues as well as male ones.

SOCIAL FLIRTING AT THE OFFICE

Social flirting in an office environment consists primarily of being a cheerful team player who makes others want to play on her team. This isn't about getting out of work. It's about doing your work, helping others do theirs, and filling in the spaces with thoughtful gestures that get you noticed.

Inevitably, personality conflicts arise in work environments but rise above them and learn to ignore the skirmishes. Instead of getting caught up in the mudslinging, focus on making yourself look good. If your colleague complains to the boss about you, compliment her strengths to the boss. Make certain that the boss knows that you volunteered to help her out on a project or you covered for her when she had to dash out on a personal crisis. Most bosses are wise; they normally don't rise to management status without the intelligence to figure out the good versus the bad. (There are exceptions. But the good news is that those who manage to escape and rise higher than their abilities are often found out, too.)

I once worked in an office with a very bright young lady. She had some good things going for her and could have been successful, except that she was extremely insecure. As a result, she spent tremendous time and energy worrying about being slighted by others. Most of the "slights" were imagined. I wish I had a dollar for every time she marched into my office for a nervous confrontation or went to the boss to undermine me. It became very frustrating until I realized that two-person battles were waging throughout the office, and the common denominator was she. Not one other person was having a problem with anyone else. It was always Sally against Mary; Sally against Jane; Sally against Beth and never Mary, Jane, or Beth against anyone else. I pointed that out to the boss who began to observe the truth in that statement. Eventually, her little ploys began to fail with management and she moved onto another job where she again caused the same problems and soon left there.

While she worked with us, though, we all got together and decided to take the high road. We bought her flowers or took her to lunch when she was having a bad day. We offered help when she got in over her head, which was often. Gradually, it became clear to management who the troublemaker was. I have often wondered what happened to her and would love to have a magic mirror that would reveal how her career has unfolded. Unless she changed her methods, she isn't a very happy person wherever she is—and those around her are certainly not happy. Don't let a person like this take you down with her. Stand tall and stand your ground.

Social flirting at the office is rooted in compassion. Approaching it from this manner will always enable you to be more understanding to someone who snaps at you or treats you unkindly. You never know what may be going on in his personal life. I once watched a usually nice guy morph into a disgruntled, ill-tempered co-worker. He became volatile, and dealing with him was like being on a roller coaster. Like most Southern women, I took and took and then I gave with the force of vengeance. I told him off to a fare-thee-well. And when my eloquent display of self-righteousness was over, his shoulders slumped and he dropped his head in his hands. He poured out his story: His wife had left him for someone else,

and a few days later, he had learned that his father was termi-
nally ill. I still feel like a low heel when I think about it. Don't
make this sad mistake. The best way to approach a situation
like that is to ask, "Is there something troubling you lately?
You haven't been yourself and, to be honest, it's been difficult
to work with you." Compassion can smooth the roughest
roads.

FLIRT ALERT:

Be nice to and cooperative with everyone at the
office. You never know who might be related to,
sleeping with, or tattling to the boss.

Significant Others Are Significant

If your boss is a man who is married, don't ever forget that
it is just as important, sometimes more so, for his wife to like
you as it for him to like you. Therefore, she can never be made
to feel intimidated or threatened. Too, women can be very in-
tuitive and keyed into things that men often miss. An em-
ployee who treats the spouse with courtesy and good manners
will gain favor, respect, and probably a good word put into the
ear of the office decision maker. Never, never underestimate
the influence that a loving, attentive wife has on her husband.
Pillow talk is powerful. It can punch you in the eye or push
you up the ladder of success. It can help or hinder your career.

One young woman I know launched a spectacular career
by using the 4-H Award-winning sewing skills of her youth.

She was at a party at her boss's house one night when his wife was fretting over a problem. They were leaving on a trip the next day, and she had forgotten to take a skirt to be hemmed. It went with a suit that she was planning to wear to an important event.

Listening attentively and spotting opportunity is a crucial skill of the savvy social flirter, particularly in a business context. The young lady, Lydia, spoke up.

"I could hem it for you. It wouldn't take long at all. I'd be happy to do it." She later said that she was offering simply out of typical Southern courtesy, without a hidden agenda at all.

The wife's eyes widened. "You can sew?"

"Yes m'am. I've been sewing since I was six when I started making clothes for my Barbie doll."

The woman waved it away. "I couldn't ask you to do that." Still, it was apparent from her eyes that she wanted to.

"I don't mind at all." Lydia set down her glass and placed her hand on the other woman's elbow. "Let's do it right now. Do you have a thread and needle?"

Within a half hour, the alteration was completed and Lydia had sewed up her future. She quickly rose through the ranks and eventually became heir-apparent to the boss. Once she managed to stand out in the crowd and get a little inside help on the home front, her ability carried her straight to success.

Business flirting has some conflicting rules, though. You can socially flirt with a female spouse but have to be mighty careful in doing the same with a male spouse. In fact, usually the last thing you want is for a husband to be bragging about you to his wife, your boss. That could be a definite setback, unless it is an unusually strong marriage between equally powerful people. If there's a power struggle in which he resents her success, his compliments of you will pick at the scab of wound.

One evening at business party, I cringed while watching a young woman who had too much to drink and too little to wear. She rubbed her well-exposed cleavage repeatedly against the arm of her boss's husband. When I saw the boss walk over, grab his other arm, and pull him away purportedly to meet someone else, I knew it was the beginning of the end. It was. Within six months, the young woman was looking for another job after repeatedly not being able to please her boss with any assignment. I knew clearly where the boss's dissatisfaction had begun. Still, you want the husband to like you, too. Just proceed with caution and use your common sense. The following are a few guidelines for dealing with spouses.

When Your Boss's Spouse Is Female:

- Touching her hand or arm is fine. It creates emotional intimacy.

- Standing close creates additional intimacy as well, but be aware if she appears uncomfortable. Everyone has a different comfort zone for closeness. Don't violate that zone.

- Conversation on family, home, and social activities works well and are good connectors for women.

- Leaning over to whisper establishes further warmth.

- Without hesitation, offer whatever advice or help you feel comfortable offering.

- Don't gossip about others in the office. It's so catty. Stay above it. What you say about others says more about you.

- Don't brag too much on her husband, although it is acceptable and wise to express admiration when appropriate.

- Don't repeat family stories he may have shared at the water cooler, especially ones that are too personal or spotlight mistakes she made. Wives tend to be more sensitive about this than husbands.

- Compliment her on her clothing, jewelry, hair, house, etc. Focus on her and talk minimally about yourself. Really get to know her.

- Look for common ground—mutual interests, shared concerns, and, if possible, humor. Remember, shared laughter creates a powerful bond.

When Your Boss's Spouse Is Male:

- Avoid most or all touching. It is okay at the appropriate time to touch his sleeve with one fingertip.

- Stand at least a foot away from him, if possible. If you're in a group, allow someone else to stand between you.

- Don't lean into his space. It could be misinterpreted by him and/or someone else across the room, like your boss.

- Converse about current events, financial news, and pop culture. The best topic is sports. Throw out something about local or national sports, get him started, and then just stand there, smile, and nod.

- Ask for his opinion. What does he think about the new traffic law or the local bank being sold to a giant corporation? Stand back and listen with interest.

- Don't gossip about others. It's unprofessional.

- Brag on his wife. It'll make him feel good (men like to be validated about their choice in partners) and he'll probably tell her, too.

- Talk about family stories your boss has shared with you. These have her seal of approval and are fine to share in a gracious way.

- Compliment him on his house, boat, motorcycle, or grill. These compliments are not too personal and don't send the wrong signal. Men love to talk about their toys.

- Ask how he met his wife. This is a great question because it underscores that you're not interested in him and gives him a personal story to tell—and will be interesting because we women always love a romantic story.

SOCIAL FLIRTING BEGINS WITH THOUGHTFUL MANNERS

It's known as common courtesy but, unfortunately, it's becoming uncommon. It is amazing how many people ignore courtesies, acting thoughtlessly or even rudely. I have friends who are never on time, often arriving fifteen minutes or more late while others don't RSVP or send thank you notes. To be honest, though, I am grateful for these backsliders on manners. Why? Because they make the rest of us, who conscientiously practice thoughtfulness, look so good. When you flirt by using courtesy, it draws positive attention to you (Southern women *love* attention. We live for it.). Isn't that nice?

If the party is at their home, always take a hostess gift

You'd be surprised how many people neglect to do this for professional gatherings. That's good for you, because it'll make you stand out in the crowd.

Be punctual

If it's a dinner party with a set time, arrive right on time. Drive around the block if you need to, but don't show up early! First, it's rude because the hosts are counting the minutes they have left for last-minute details. Second, you'll be forced to chitchat and it's more difficult until the party atmosphere gets going.

Know when to leave

Don't outstay your welcome. Go home. You never want to be the last to leave.

Offer high praise

Compliment their home, garden, food, family photos, pets, or children. In social flirting, compliments are the foundation on which all goodwill is built. It enables others to tear down walls and let you in.

Be gracious and precious

Be as gracious and nice to servers, bartenders, and staff as you are to the hosts. Do a little social flirting with them. Smile broadly, wink sweetly, and thank them profusely. Most people who become very successful in life get there by treating employees with respect. As a result, these kinds of people listen to the opinions of those they pay. If you stand out in a good way—or bad—there's a chance they'll share that information with their employer.

Use good sense

Dress appropriately, even after hours. It is possible to be elegantly sexy, which is fine. Promiscuously sexy isn't.

Say yes or no

For goodness sake: RSVP! So many people don't. How rude. It gets social flirting off to a bad start. Set the stage for terrific flirting by responding promptly to invitations.

Use more good sense

Never take of someone's hospitality and then harshly criticize it afterward. It's ungracious to hosts who have put time and money into an event, plus many times it gets back to them through the grapevine.

Be appropriately repentant

If you spill something like red wine, you owe the hostess an extra gift. Send flowers the next day with an apology.

Remember to send a handwritten thank you note the next day

No e-mail thank you's! If the party was at their home, mail it. If it was onsite at the office, drop it in internal mail or leave it on her chair while she's gone to lunch.

HOW TO GET AHEAD AT THE OFFICE BY SOCIALLY FLIRTING:

Use the power of the spoken word

Always say, "Thank you," "I appreciate you," or "I owe you one."

Show respect

Ask, don't demand. Even if you're the boss, ask rather than command. It goes a long way in building relationships. When I was sixteen, I worked for a guy who would always end an assignment by saying, "If you don't mind, ma'am. Thank you." I have never forgotten that. I would have walked through fire for him.

Use the power of the written word

Send notes of appreciation. Pick up a pen and write a note to a coworker or your boss, expressing gratitude or praise. Or e-mail one and copy others on it. I have often left notes on keyboards and telephones.

Make gestures of kindness

If your boss's assistant is swamped and can't go to lunch, offer to pick something up for her. If a coworker's child is sick and she needs to leave, offer to catch her phone. If someone's car is in the shop, offer a ride. If you have excellent computer skills and a colleague doesn't, offer your technical expertise on a project, even if it means staying late one night.

No big "I's" and little "You's"

Treat everyone with equal courtesy and kindness. That way you can do thoughtful gestures for the boss and the boss's boss without being accused of brownnosing. (A big wink between us on that!)

Hide and don't seek company

Hide away on bad days. We can't all be nice every minute of every day. Sometimes a fight with your spouse that morning can ruin your mood. In that case, stay at your desk or cubicle and bury your head in work. Others do not deserve to be treated with discourtesy because of your personal woes.

Be in the know

Make it a policy to know the assistant of every manager or executive. These assistants are powerful. Use your conversation skills to chat them up and become friendly. Be careful with the information you acquire, though. Don't share it with others. If you do, it will be all over the office in no time.

Play hostess

Host an office gathering, such as a cookout, at your house. It takes initiative to do this and bosses look highly on those who are assertive. Besides, social gatherings of this kind allow colleagues to bond in very strong ways (especially with the charming hostess).

Listen for hints

If a coworker or your boss mentions something of particular interest to her, always keep an eye open for it. For instance, if one collects hat pins and you run across one at a yard sale, buy it as a gift. It won't cost much but its results will be priceless.

Be interested in others' problems, promotions, and personal particulars such as children, church, etc. The best way to establish yourself in someone's good graces is to care about what they care about.

Be exuberant

The most skillful decorate business flirting as beautiful as a handmade bow on a birthday gift. People gravitate toward those who smile, sparkle, and entertain cheerfully. Practice your storytelling—we Southerners use a lot of descriptive words—and enthrall people with that talent over lunch, coffee breaks, or at social gatherings. *Simple fact is that bosses promote people they like, sometimes over more qualified candidates.* One reason women have struggled to break through the glass ceiling is that the bosses were often promoting their buddies, especially their golfing pals. It wasn't deliberate gender discrimination but rather unintentional social discrimination because women didn't assert themselves to break into that social inner circle. That's one of the greatest benefits of social flirting in the professional arena. It opens the doors for women to be part of the buddy system.

FLIRT ALERT:

It takes a lot of work to build your credibility with others, but sixty seconds of bad judgment can destroy it all. Be careful not to break one word of a confidence.

I'll conclude this chapter with two brief anecdotes of social flirting in the professional world, one serious and the other light-hearted. As a young sportswriter, I filed a story from a ball game one night then left the stadium. I needed to pick up a fresh notepad for the next day's game so I ran by the newspaper's office. When I came into the empty newsroom, I noticed that the light was on in the publisher's officer, very unusual for midnight on a Friday. I walked across the hall and was met by the publisher who had stumbled to the door. As he fell into my arms, I saw that his face was covered in blood. I dialed 911 then called his wife, who arrived frantic. They were new in town and knew virtually no one, so I drove her to the hospital and stayed with her all night until we learned that he had blacked out, hit his head severely when he fell and his glasses had broken, cutting his face in several places. Genuine compassion and thoughtfulness scored me two new friends and powerful allies. When the boss was out of town, his wife would take me to brunch after church. Then, when the paper's executive editor decided he would cover a major bowl game in a glamorous city, despite the fact that I had been covering the team all year long in podunk small Southern towns, guess who stepped in? And guess who got to go to the glamorous bowl game? Not the executive editor, that's for sure.

One South Carolina friend, Mary, earned a college summer internship by flirting with some journalists on a hotel elevator during a Sigma Delta Chi convention in Buffalo, New York. She was representing the University of South Carolina student chapter, so her name tag identified her as a broadcasting major. The managing editor of a metropolitan daily newspaper, who was one who was being flirted with, asked, "Why would a smart girl like you pursue a career in TV instead of newspaper journalism?"

Mary batted her eyelashes, then asked with a wink and smile, "Why don't you hire me for the summer and give me a chance to change my mind?"

He did. Right on the spot. Another successful case of social flirting in the business world.

Courtship Flirting

CHAPTER SEVEN

THE BELLE RINGS AND
ROMANCE ANSWERS

I was working out at a health club one day when an old friend wandered over to ask a question.

"How is it that Southern women can flirt with you and you never know you're being flirted with?" Charlie, handsome and successful, had been divorced for several months, and apparently had been blindsided by a few well-accomplished, exquisitely trained flirts.

I put down the weights, tilted my head, and asked, "You can't tell when you're being flirted with?"

He shook his head and, obviously perplexed, wrinkled his brow. "Not when it's a Southern woman. Other women are bolder and more outright with their intentions. It's easy to see. But I can't see what's going on when a Southern woman flirts with me."

Beautiful. That's exactly how it should be. A man should not see it coming, realize what's happening while it's going on, or know what hit him when it's gone. Like the scent of honeysuckle on a hot summer's day, ladylike flirtation should linger lightly in the air and stay gently on a man's mind after she drifts softly away. It should be as subliminal as the advertisements in movie theaters that drive you straight toward the popcorn. Since you think it was your idea, you happily plunk down the money. When a man answers the irresistible call of a lovely siren, he enjoys it much more when it's "his" idea.

"It is impossible for me to tell when you women are flirting with me," complained another male friend over dinner. "It's so subtle that I don't have a clue what's going on. Women over fifty are a little more overt in their flirting but the younger ones—oh, the younger ones are almost secretive about it!"

Both of these men are very successful and smart. They didn't accomplish all they have by being dumb. But both, planted firmly in the deep heart of Dixie, have definitely met their matches when it comes to the flirtatious exploits of Southern female charmers. They're both in way over their cute little heads and that's just the way it should be. Bless their hearts.

My friend Sharon is beautiful and flirts with everyone, especially her husband of many years. I was in the car with them one day when another car pulled out suddenly and Pearce, her husband, almost hit it.

"Oh, honey! What are you doing?" Sharon squealed.

"It wasn't my fault," he said in a nice tone. "That other car just came from outta nowhere."

She patted him on the shoulder. "Darling, I wasn't talking to you. I was talking to that other guy." She turned to me and winked. "See there. He knows his name: Honey. He thought I was talking to him."

Southern women love to use terms of endearment such as Darling, Sweet Dear, Honey, Sweetie Pie, and Precious. We believe in tea that's sweet and words that are sweeter. We even distinguish between milk by referring to it as buttermilk and sweet milk and the gentle command of "Give me some sugar," is an invitation for a kiss, not to pass the sugar bowl. Southern mamas know the power of sweet. That's why most mamas, like mine, have two parting words for their daughters as they leave the house for a date or a trip—"Be sweet." Not, mind you, "be careful" but "be sweet." In their minds, being sweet takes precedence over not being in an accident. Plus, they know that the best way to capture a guy's attention is to "be sweet." Sweetness is the nectar of Dixie divas who know that more flies are captured in a small jar of honey than in a big ol' tub of vinegar.

It's easier to call a member of the opposite sex by a term of endearment if you practice using pet nicknames on everyone. It becomes so natural that it just rolls off your tongue with that special him. I regularly call friends and children, "Sweetie," and my dog, "Baby." I coo to her constantly. Then, when I flirt with a guy, it sounds and feels absolutely right— to him and to me—to casually throw out a sweet name. Guys love this. They melt at a perfectly placed endearment but only if it doesn't sound awkward. A key to great courtship flirting is a comfortable ease with words and gestures.

"I call everybody 'darlin'," Merri Grace admits. "It especially helps when I can't remember a name so I just say, 'Why, hey there, darlin'! How are you?' That person never knows I forgot his name because I use it for everyone."

Men love to be *babied*, and they love to be called *"baby."* *Just remember this:* You can never brag on them too much or sweet talk them too much. It is impossible. In the South, sweet words and nicknames are a comfortable part of our culture, but I realize that it isn't as comfortable in all regions. So, just work on it and gradually add it into your conversation and personality. Eventually, it'll feel right as rain and bring about results as beautiful as the Virginia coast on a clear evening.

FLIRT ALERT:

Light his fire by leaning over and breathily saying, "Oh baby, I'm so happy to see you. I've missed you terribly." Finish it with a tiny pout and slight flutter. Men melt like homemade ice cream in July when they're called "baby."

THE CHASE BEGINS

Once a man is interested, he will initiate the chase so settle back and wait for the troops to advance. Don't, don't, don't advance on him because immediate retreat will occur, and you will have lost the battle before it begins. It is important to use subtlety in romance while executing the dance to the point that it's a beautiful waltz. Men are born to be hunters. They thrive on it even in our modern world. At the beginning of time, long before refined sugar and flour, men went out and proudly hunted down their game. All men love the thrill of the chase, and it carries over into every aspect of their lives, including romance. If a woman is too easy to bag—or in this case: bed—they lose interest almost immediately. But a woman who brings a man along slowly with a wink and promise, who allows him to really get to know her and fall solidly in love with her before the relationship becomes intimate, stands a much higher chance of keeping him for good.

"If you want to win a boy," Mama always said, "keep him guessing." How true, how true. Trust me, this approach works. I regularly get cards, flowers, e-mails, and calls as well as notes left on my car that all say essentially the same thing: "Since I met you, I can't stop thinking about you." Women who chase men steal the thrill from them so the guys are bored easily and quickly move on elsewhere. They keep drifting until they find a woman who allows herself to be chased. Be sure to wear stilettos, though. You don't want to run too fast, and you definitely want to look good while he's hot on your four-inch heels!

FLIRT ALERT:

Marketing is key to selling anything, including yourself. Package yourself to sell.

HOT CHICKS AND COOL WAYS

How do you get a guy to chase you in the first place? First, *attract* his attention, then *capture* his attention, then *escape* his attention. When handled correctly, you'll soon be getting *all* of his attention.

Attract His Attention

Femininity covers Dixie like the dew. Southern women celebrate our femininity with softness and allure. We also know that flirting works best when the marketing package is beautiful and eye-catching. Here are some of the essential attention-attracting magnets that every woman should have:

Chat Makers—It is imperative to always have something that will allow a guy to sidle up and start a conversation. You may naturally possess it, like a gorgeous mane of Rapunzel-like hair; but if you don't, create it: a piece of unique jewelry, a pair of stunning high heels, an attention-grabbing belt, leather slacks, or a bright-colored jacket.

Color Counts—Southern divas know that bright colors attract more attention than a redheaded woman in a room full of blond-headed men. We're still not that sure about white wedding dresses. Why can't wedding dresses be red or hot pink? Play toys for children, especially educational toys, are always brightly colored in vivid primary tones. The reason is simple: Children are attracted to stunning color, and it keeps their attention. That's the kind of attractions we never outgrow—as adults, we continue to be drawn to the vibrancy.

All Made Up—Non-Southern women never understand our absolute infatuation with makeup. It's true that Southern divas never leave the house, even to run to the corner convenience store, without the full arraignment of mascara, lipstick, blush, and dark circle concealer. You know why that's important? It's part of the packaging, and every marketer knows that packaging is one of the critical aspects of selling a product. How you prepare the packaging reveals how you feel about the contents. If you decorate the package well, it shows a lot of pride about what is inside.

Hair Affair—Of course you know that hair is very important to Dixie darlings. It is so obvious that sometimes it is the subject of television shows. I met a young man who was working on his doctorate degree from a California university and was doing his thesis on social culture of the South. I asked what he had learned during the months he had been plopped down in the midst of the South. "Well," he started with a grin, "you women have this thing with your hair. There's this beauty queen hair that you gals want." He reached over and touched my hair. "You've got it." I was glad he noticed. I was also amused that a sociologist came to study the South and our hair was his chief observation! Hair that has movement, shiny color, and at least some length is eye-catching to both men and women. As with makeup, our hair says something strong about each of us. It points out our individuality. It is the bow on top of the package.

Personal Investment—The money you spend on yourself in the form of good clothes, manicures, and a good hairstylist is an investment in the most important commodity you possess—yourself. It's money well spent because it increases your price or "resale" value. I have paid outrageous prices for darling high heels but found that the money was well spent. Prissing goes much better in expensive heels! When you feel richly adorned, you walk worthy.

Short Cuts—If you've got great legs, wear a short skirt. If you don't, you can be just as sexy in a long skirt, especially if it's cut on the bias.

Dressing the Part—Yes, what you wear matters. It sure does to our darling divas. But what might surprise you is that size doesn't matter in terms of sex appeal. Despite the fact that weight is a constant struggle in our land of fried plenty, size doesn't matter—but *attitude* about size matters mightily. Unfortunately, some women get depressed over weight gain and then cease to care about their appearance. Their hair is always in disarray; they abandon makeup, manicures, and pedicures and they give no thought to clothes, other than throwing something on that billows enough to cover the poundage. It is that display of carelessness that turns the situation into sex-repeal instead of sex appeal. You don't have to be a size six to get attention from a guy, just dressed in a fetching manner. After all, it's called *sex* appeal, not *six* appeal.

Burden of Proof—Prove to him that you need him. Allow him to carry your luggage, boxes, bags, mascara, whatever. Men like to be needed. It revs their engines. If he doesn't offer, thrust the bundle into his arms and say, "You're so sweet. Thank you so much."

Little Things Count—Southern divas know that paying attention to the little details goes a long way in the art of flirting. It says that nothing is too small to slip by you and that goes a long way in selling yourself. The perfect earrings, a lovely fragrance, the right shoes (you know they have to match the outfit!), even the perfect color of hosiery are of critical importance.

Men notice first the women who have put time into their appearance. Guys are very visual and are drawn by that before anything else. These days, fewer and fewer women take time to take care of themselves, but that makes the odds better for those of us who do. One of my friends from New England was visiting; one morning she came bounding down the stairs and nonchalantly informed me, "Sorry kiddo, but I'm not wearing makeup today." She rarely wears makeup so I'm not sure why she even bothered to address it, other than she was in the land of perfectly appointed divas.

I took a sip of coffee. "Fine," I responded, clearly unruffled. This got her attention and she asked, "Really? You don't *care* if I don't wear makeup?"

"Not at all," I said with a sweet smile. "This way *I'll* get all of the attention and I won't have to share any with *you*. So why would I mind?"

Wordlessly, she turned around, marched right back upstairs, and put on her makeup.

Capture His Attention—Once you've entered a room, all adorned and suddenly all adored, he will find a way to speak to you. This is where you set about mesmerizing and capti-

vating. Here are some important tips for subtly capturing his
attention:

Shut the Cell Up—The person you're talking to, face to face,
should have your undivided attention. Period. In social situations, turn your cell phone off and leave it in your purse. Shut
it down before you enter the room.

AVAILABLE TO BE CHASED

First and foremost, you must let him know that you are available and interested. Come up with a funny little story or wit-
ticism that expresses your interest. Find a way to do it so that
it reveals something about you so that you can connect
quickly and flirt proficiently. Here are a couple of stories I
field-tested while working on this book:

> Guy: "So, what's your occupation?"
> Me: "I'm a writer."
> Guy: "Really? What do you write?"
> Me: "Right now, I'm working on a book about flirting."
> Guy with a chuckle: "Flirting?"
> Me with a coquettish smile and slight eyelash flutter:
> "Yes, and I'm looking for volunteers for my research.
> Interested?"

In speaking engagements when I mentioned this book on
flirting, I always joked, "My mama said, 'If you're such an expert then why aren't you married?' " The audience would in-

evitably start laughing and with a coquettish look, I always said, "That's why I'm such an expert. I get a lot of practice!" Without fail, I always had several men approach me later and began a conversation by saying with a smile, "I'm not married either." *Remember: Nothing works better in flirtation than humor, especially when used in a self-effacing manner. It makes you more approachable.*

One friend signals her availability by saying, "You know, you remind me in looks of my most recent ex-boyfriend. But don't worry, that's a good thing. I like the way he looked just not the way he kissed. Especially when he was kissing another woman!"

Personality's A Plus—Developing an ease with people and conversing comfortably with them is a huge selling point, and a woman with a funny, smart, warm personality is hugely sexy. Some are born with naturally wonderful personalities. Most, myself included, aren't. Southern divas, though, know that these skills can be learned. Do some test marketing. Try different techniques and find what works with people. Here's the first tip—*nice works*.

Smart Is Sexy—Intellectual stimulation is as important as physical stimulation. Smart men are drawn to smart women. You do want a smart man, don't you? The key is not to be overwhelming with your smarts because guys will skitter away from you. It's terrific to be super smart, but some things we need to keep to ourselves. Otherwise, we intimidate others, and that's not gracious behavior. Celebrate your smartness, just don't smother guys with too much of it. The best approach is to ask a lot of questions about him. Men, because of their storied strong persona, are too often neglected by women who don't realize the importance of getting him to talk about himself. Male or female, we all have an emotional need to be of interest to others. The most successful femme fatales know exactly how to get a man keenly attracted: Have him talk about himself.

Be Scent-suous—Nothing is more sensuous to a man when a woman is fully clothed than the sensual seduction of her scent. Perfume will be one of your most important selling points. Be sure to layer it from lotion to powder to perfume. A beautiful fragrance will linger long after you part his company and make you unforgettable.

Escape His Attention

Men aren't reasonable about romance like we are. Women meet a guy, know there's a connection, and that's that. But men, goodness gracious, they have to have a *challenge*. This is completely subconscious for men. They don't even realize this aggravating propensity while women rarely want to accept that it exists. This is where trouble usually starts between the opposite sexes. As is our nature, we women want to nurture, comfort, and cuddle; but what we must do is play it cool. Here's how to practice the part:

Set It Up, Then Walk Away—When you meet him, do all the aforementioned. Plant yourself deeply in his mind. Do not let yourself get emotionally entangled at this point because it will only trip you up as you navigate this blind path. Do make certain that he knows of a way to contact you. Do this subtly by mentioning the name of the company where you work or by making a point of talking about a mutual friend. If he's interested, he'll find you. Don't worry about that.

Don't Contact Him—Whatever it takes, do not make the first contact. Guys are so used to this in today's society that he will immediately lump you with all the other gals who are desperate to date him. Stand out in the crowd by lying in wait. It may be hard, but it will bring the best results. Otherwise, you will be starting the relationship at a disadvantage. From the beginning, you must strive to maintain the upper hand.

Keep Your Distance—Do not have any physical contact with him the first two to three times that you see him. No hand holding, no kissing, and most certainly nothing more intimate. Too many females give up too much too early. Wrong! Remember the idea of the chase and the hunt? The quicker the chase ends, the quicker the romance ends. The entire concept is based on keeping his interest high enough that he gets to know you and, of course, cannot resist falling in love with you. Too much physical involvement also dangerously plays with your self-esteem, especially if he never calls back. Do not let any guy have this kind of power over you. Protect your self-worth at all costs, knowing that high self-esteem will take you to whatever you want in life.

I have a strong rule for myself about dating: I don't hike, bike, or kiss on the first date. Seriously. To me, kissing is reserved for those to whom I feel emotionally or intimately connected. To share it essentially with a stranger feels odd. It also isn't special. Guys want to feel special, even more than they want to feel an orgasm. Hard to believe, but it's true. In the short run of about two minutes, they want an orgasm—but in the long run, they want to feel special to you. This is where the art of flirting is most important. Entice him, intrigue him, make him feel that he is the most desired man in the world, but do it by limiting physical contact. *Courtship flirting is all about playing the game of romance without taking your clothes off.*

Exercise Smart Restraint—If he asks for your phone number, give him only your home number or if you're not completely comfortable, give him your e-mail address. Do not give him your cell number because that makes you appear too accessible. I have two phones at home. One is the number I put on my personal cards. Often, those calls go into voicemail. The other number is very private and reserved for closer friends. Same with e-mail: I have a private address and a more public one. Make the guy work his way into your closer circle: Start with e-mail; then go to your phone number; then, after some time, give out your cell number. Guys love this! It shows them that they're making progress. It's rewarding to the hunter. Also, when he does contact you, either by e-mail or voice mail, don't grab the opportunity to immediately respond. Wait at least twenty-four hours, then respond by explaining that you've been so busy that you're just getting a moment to answer. Guys love this, too, because it increases the adventure and signals that you're not the clingy type. Clingy women are a nightmare every man wants to avoid; they kill the chase and replace it with its opposite—a woman that men want to run from.

Calling Cards—In the South, we have always favored calling cards, especially important to non-career women who do not have business cards. Also, you don't want a personal interest calling you at work. It could jeopardize your job; plus, you can't be coy and intriguingly flirtatious from your office phone like you can on your home phone. Have some pretty cards printed up on colored stock—these will stick out beautifully in his billfold of white or cream cards—and put on them whatever contact information you feel comfortable giving out. For example, I use a post office address, not my street address in order to ward off unwanted visitors at my front door. List an e-mail address and/or your phone number. Besides convenience, another benefit is that when you give a card to a guy, it's less personal and makes him feel like he is being treated like hoards of other potential suitors. This makes the hunt more thrilling, and keeps that monstrous male ego from going nuts.

Here's how the cards work: I met a cute, eligible doctor and we chatted for several minutes when, suddenly, I said, "Let me give you my card." I dug into my purse, pulled it out, and handed it to him. "You should be careful, giving me your card," he said smiling. "I might use it to call and ask you out."

I smiled back and winked. "Why do you think I gave it to you?"

Patience Prevails—Whatever it takes, don't give in and start calling and e-mailing him. And don't be discouraged if it takes a while for him to fall into calling you on a regular basis. This is typically male. While we might be thinking and longing for them, they're all caught up in game scores, where to eat lunch, and the latest stock prices. But rest assured that there does come a time—and it's different with each guy—when he suddenly thinks of you and realizes that he hasn't heard from you. This drives all of them crazy. This is when you stand out in the crowd, and that's what you want. If you have set this up right by letting him know you're interested and then by not harassing him, he will be back. Always. I got an e-mail to my Web site from a reader who explained that her great love had just broken up with her, moved away, and said he needed time. She was crazed and asked what to do. I warned her, "Do not, whatever you do, contact him in any way. Give him time, and he'll be back." She suffered but she stuck it out and never contacted him. I thought it would take months, but three weeks later, he called to tell her that he couldn't live without her. He moved back and they got married. Just remember that men do not possess our instinct and intuition and, therefore, it takes them longer to figure out things than it takes us. Poor dears.

Set the Standard—A guy will treat you the best he's ever going to treat you in the beginning of a relationship, when he's on his best behavior. After a while, he starts the slide. The South is predominantly a matriarchal society where women rule, albeit gently. We Dixie divas know that we have to take control and guide the treatment we receive from the beginning. Do not let a guy mistreat you by not keeping his word, canceling a date at the last minute, or disrespecting you in any way. If any of this happens, tell him firmly what you expect, always keeping in mind that there are plenty of guys out there looking for a good, decent woman like you. Now is not the time to be mealymouthed. It's the time to be strong and self-assured in a nondominating way. Don't ever forget that the beginning of a relationship sets the tone for what's to come. If he has disrespected you in any way such as not being courteous and prompt, when he calls, let him suffer by not taking his call. And don't return it, either. Men can't stand to be ignored. He'll probably wait a few days or even a few weeks and then call again. If you're inclined to talk to him, wait a couple of days and return the call. Chances are that he'll be ready to reform, so make it hard for him to get back into your good graces. If he doesn't call a second time, good riddance. Don't waste your time and energy on a dysfunctional relationship.

The Too Rule—The best way to tell a guy that you love him is, "I love you, *too*." Even if you have to cajole and tickle it out of him, it's best—for you and your relationship—if he says it first and you respond to it. Those three words scare a guy mightily if he hears them before he feels them. *Remember: Men move at a much slower pace emotionally than women. You have to make allowances for that.*

Mama Knows Best—Nobody knows your guy better than his mother. Make friends with her and learn all she knows: his dislikes, childhood memories, favorite things, the recipes for his most beloved food. In the battle for his heart and his left ring finger, she will be your greatest ally or your worst enemy. Not only does she know her boy, but she also has his ear and can influence him greatly—toward you or away from you.

Breaking the Ice: Ask the Right Questions

Getting through to someone means getting to know him. If you ask the right questions and listen to your instincts, you'll be right on target. Each the following three sections provide five questions to ask when you're at different levels of intimacy.

Initial Chitchat

When you meet a guy, get him to talk about himself. This enables you to know him better—plus when you listen closely, you'll know what to reveal about yourself. If you find out that he's a staunch Republican, don't bring up that you worked for Young Democrats when you were in college. Some things are best revealed later in the relationship. Here are some introductory, small-talk questions to draw him out:

Five Questions to Break the Ice.

- What's your occupation? Is that what you've always wanted to do?

- Where did you go to college? Why did you choose that school?

- What's your favorite sports team? (Guys can talk forever about that and they love it when a gal asks.)

- Who do you know best in this room? (This helps you know how you're going to get your contact information to him if he doesn't ask or how you're going to set up another chance meeting with him.)

- What's your favorite ice cream? (This one is so unusual that it really starts a conversation going. He'll probably wonder aloud why you would ask such a question. Tell him it reveals a lot about a person's personality. Do it, of course, in a very teasing, lighthearted way. If you want to flirt more boldly, say with a smile and a wink, "I can tell how good a kisser a guy will be by the flavor he chooses!" *One word of caution:* Be wary of guys who pick vanilla as their favorite flavor. That usually means little adventure or fun with that one!)

Moving Closer

By the second date, you'll want to know more about him. Over dinner, a few well-thought-out questions will take you closer to the person he is. *One word of warning:* Be prepared for him not to know these answers. I once asked a date what his favorite color was and he looked at me as if I had asked him for the formula to the atomic bomb! Don't worry, though. He'll go away and think about it, and in the process, you will introduce him to himself as well as to you. He will be more drawn to a woman who is so interested in him that she asks questions that he hadn't even thought of. He'll realize there's something very special about you.

Five Questions To Ask When You're Really Getting to Know Someone

- How long have you been friends with your oldest friends? (This is the biggest key to understanding how he deals with relationships. If he has had the same best friends for many years, then he is grounded, reasonable, approachable, and not scared to commit. If he doesn't have any close friends, be very wary. It probably means that he's difficult in relationships and/or he's built up walls to prevent others from getting close to him. This is good to know up front.)

- As a child, what was your favorite game of pretend? (Our childhood fantasy games reveal the desires of our hearts and what we are really meant to pursue in life. Playing as a cowboy shows that he wants to be rugged and manly. If he played being a banker and then grew up to work in the financial services industry, then he probably has an inner peace and no conflict about going in the wrong direction career-wise).

- Are you closer to your mom or dad? (This reveals which parent influenced his upbringing more and will also open him up to start sharing stories such as a fishing trip with his dad or his mom's guidance on his education. A strong, healthy respect for his mom will mean that he has that kind of respect for other women.)

- How many houses did you live in as a child? (This indicates his level of stability or versatility. It will also open up more family information such as whether his parents are divorced, etc.)

• Who did you vote for in the last presidential election? (Political party choices are important in determining if you match up well philosophically.)

Up Close and Personal

As the relationship progresses, you need to look deeper into the soul of this person. It's amazing to me how many people are married and don't know the answer to the five questions that follow. Listen closely to these answers because they will give you a road map for how to relate to him in a more intimate way. You'll also discover whether it's a road you *want* to travel.

FLIRT ALERT:

As the relationship deepens, never hesitate to use the wink that grows up to be a flutter. Southern women are experts at fluttering, which is the rapid winking of both eyes done in brief succession. Done subtly, it's extremely feminine. Exaggerate it for a lighthearted comic moment. Either way, fluttering is flattering: to him and for you.

Five Questions to Ask When You're Ready to Establish Emotional Intimacy

- When and where were you the happiest in your life? (If he says as a child surrounded by his family and their love, you're on the road to finding a great husband. If he says it was in college where he partied all the time with his fraternity, then be very forewarned!)

- If you could change one thing in your life, what would it be?

- What's your greatest fear? (Be gentle when asking this one. Men hate to admit such things, but when they do, it's a tremendous emotional release as well as a strong bonding with you.)

- What has been your biggest heartache? (This will offer a major clue for understanding how he reacts to disappointments and loss.)

- Who is your hero? (This will open up the discussion for what traits and attitudes he admires in a person. Listen closely.)

Don't forget that all successful flirting starts with strong conversation, which always starts with solid questions. To be a natural flirt, start with being naturally nosey. I don't know about you, but I'm actually quite good at that! Develop your inner sleuth, ask the right questions, and, above all, pay close attention to the answers!

CHAPTER EIGHT

SCORING WITH SPORTS

At a holiday supper, several Southern divas and our menfolk were enjoying a conversation of tremendous importance; the upcoming college football bowl games. Each woman discussed the game with an incredible wealth of knowledge, adding as much to the dialogue as the men whom, as you might imagine, were well pleased to be associated with such interesting females. Miranda ran down the list of players on one team, pointing out the strengths and weaknesses of each, and then noted that the opposing team was known for its superb running game. That could be a problem, she commented, since the other team's defensive line was riddled with injuries.

Miranda, barely a teenager, is a lovely little flirter still on training wheels. But thanks to her mom and grandmothers, her training began at an early age. At seven, she could name the entire Atlanta Braves baseball team, each guy's number, and field position. These days, she studies the sports pages as diligently as she practices her cheerleading moves. She is what we, in the South, like to call an exceptionally well-rounded young lady.

FLIRT ALERT:

Knowing about sex gets a man; knowing about sports keeps him.

Southern women are raised with an appreciation for sports, particularly Southeastern Conference football. It is amazing to see magnificently attired Southern women turn out for a football game on a muggy, steamy day in Louisiana or a rainy, chilly one in Kentucky. High heels, skirts, off-the-shoulder sweaters, even hats turn these women into a more fetching spectacle than a ninety-yard run. The football game is the circumstance, the women are the pomp and glory.

In the days of courtship, nothing is more effective in gaining favor with a new beau than playing along with his love for sports. In sustaining a relationship that follows, *nothing says romance to a man more than a woman who will share his interest in sports.* Now, this doesn't mean that you have to watch endless ball games with him—guys like to have "guy time," too—but it does mean an end to complaining about his love for it. "Playing the field" this way is exactly what courtship flirting is all about. If you play it smartly, you won't be playing the field any longer because you'll win the championship trophy: the man himself.

How To Play on His Team

Men are serious about their sports, and if a woman wants him to be serious about her, she gets serious about sports, too. In the South, we're raised on the belief that it isn't a bit unlady-like to know a touchdown from a home run or to be able to rattle off the starting lineup of our favorite team. We know that we can maintain our perfectly appointed femininity while playing the field. After all, choosing an outfit for a Clemson vs. South Carolina game is as critical as choosing the perfect wedding dress! Every Dixie darling knows that. Being sports literate increases our appeal to the opposite sex, because if there is anything that is more of aphrodisiac than red sexy lingerie, it's a woman who knows the score. Literally. A properly trained Southern woman would never admit, let alone brag, that she knew nothing about sports. She'd rather wear stockings with a run in them than say any such!

Part of the charm of courtship flirting comes from knowing the importance of having a broad base of knowledge and experience. Women who are incredibly alluring to others, es-pecially men, are magnetic because they give so much of themselves. They put an effort into learning about the things that interest others. That selfless participation in society is enormously appealing to others. It creates a connection be-tween people. Someone has to make the effort to make that connection and you can pretty well be assured that it isn't going to be the men. You have to stand ready and willing to go the distance, even if it means going all the way while the men push back in the recliner and watch the game. It takes work to be outstanding at courtship flirting, but it's well worth it.

My mentor, Mississippi-born Virgie, like all good Southern women, knows the importance of playing along. Her husband owns a race team, and where the team goes, *he* goes—and where he goes, *she* goes. "Honey," she purrs in a syrupy drawl, "if you don't go, someone else will. I'm not giving any woman that kind of opportunity to get to my man!"

Here are some pointers for scoring points with a sports-minded man.

Level the Playing Field

Sports talk is the great equalizer in conversation. It's always current and isn't as dark as many current news events tend to be. Men who are in cautious guard at the beginning of a date or a business meeting will immediately relax and let down that guard when you begin to talk about sports. Once the guard is down, you can begin to connect.

Score Big

Sports talk elicits passion and once that passion is unleashed, it's a short stroll to the next kind of passion. Men get fired up about their teams, and even if they're mad about the way the team's been playing lately, they care enough to get riled up about it. It's like a spark plug helping fire the engine. Finding a woman willing to talk sports and watch them further ignites his passion. If you're in an intimate relationship with him, be sure to have the red lingerie fired up and ready to leave the starting line.

Be a Top Recruit

If you're looking for a way to stand out in a crowd of single females, a crowd that outnumbers single men, this is it. You'd be surprised at how small the percentage is of women who are smart enough to play this game. Those who do, not only find a boyfriend, but are actively recruited to *be* a girlfriend. Before leaving for a night out, grab a look at the sports page. When dressing for a date, listen to a television sports channel. It's just as important as choosing the perfect lip gloss (and any decent diva will tell you that the perfect lip gloss is critical).

Make a Suite Deal

No man will turn down a date with a woman who has good seats (suite tickets are an aphrodisiac) to a ball game (season tickets will probably land you an engagement ring). If he does, he has a wife hiding somewhere or he's playing on the other team.

THE BIG LEAGUES

How to Play the Game

The rules are simple. In fact, you can write your own rules for the most part. Here, though, are some basics for becoming a superstar player.

Know Which Season It Is

No, it's not fall. It's *football season*. That's how men think.
April isn't spring. It's the beginning of baseball. Think and
speak in those terms.

Know the Names of the Ball Teams in Your City

In the South, minor league baseball is big but since the Atlanta
Braves was the only southern Major League team for many
years, the majority of men follow them. Do your homework
on *your* region—then show off what you've learned.

Memorize the Names of Key Players

The star scorer on the basketball team, the quarterback, the
All-Star pitcher. Then learn something personal and interesting about each one. Pick a piece of information that will
blow his mind that you know: where the player went to
school, his position in the draft, his hometown, his current
record, etc. Know something that you can throw out in a
conversation with the guy you meet while you're out dancing. Just try this once and it will become your favorite
weapon for disarming a man. It's worth all the work when
you see that look of utter fascination mingled with admiration and surprise. It is that one moment when love begins to
spark in his heart.

Find Out What His Favorite Sport Is

Then, learn the basic rules. Don't clutter your mind with the details and complexities of the sport. He'll be so thrilled that you know what it takes to score that he'll soon be trying his hand at scoring with you.

Always Know Something About Golf

Most men play golf, and if they don't play, they watch it. If you spend more time learning about just one sport, make it golf.

Emotional Connection

Women connect on any subject through emotion so use yours to get interested in sports. Look at the personal information about the players—is he the father of a physically or emotionally challenged child? Did he go into the military and then go to college and then into pro ball? That's quite a story in a society where good players leave college early to play ball. As women, we love a good story, such as the baseball manager who spends his free time with a twin brother who is dying of cancer or as a big brother to an orphaned child. Find those stories and you'll find your niche. Or, if all else fails, pick out the cutest guy with the cutest behind on the team and root for him. Whatever it takes to get you going, do it.

Prepare Your Game Plan

On Fridays and Mondays, read the sports section of *USA Today*. It gives a great synopsis of what is going to happen over the weekend and then what does happen. Save Friday's section with its predictions or expectations and compare it to Monday's results. You don't have to read the entire section but read the first paragraph of most of the stories. It'll give you a lot of what you need to know. If time is short, read the brief section that runs down the side of the first page and gives quick takes of important stories. You can even clip the briefs out, tuck them into your purse, and if you need some ammunition over the weekend, excuse yourself to the ladies' room and take a quick look.

A Little Is a Lot

It's necessary to know only enough to start a conversation. Once a man gets started on the sport of his choice, there's no stopping him. All you have to do then is keep the conversation going with questions and comments.

Pose Your Questions Carefully

Ask them in a smart way that shows you're interested but not stupid. Don't ask, "Now, what does it mean when they throw a red flag on the football field?" Instead, say, "Football can be so complex with all of its rules. Which rule do you think is the most puzzling?" Men love to answer questions, especially when they're asked in a thoughtful and meaningful way.

They're less interested in a woman who is just "playing along" and trying to act intrigued. Trust me, though, a man will take a woman who is sincerely or mildly interested or pretending to be interested. Any interest in sports will work like a magical love potion.

Scoring Points

To get a man's attention at the pool or on a plane, have a copy of *Sports Illustrated* handy. When you see a cute guy close by, grab it up and look intensely interested. It is also useful to cover what you may really be reading—*InStyle*. On a plane, don't hesitate to ask the cute guy across the aisle if you can borrow the sports section to his newspaper. You'll be surprised how well that works!

Here are a few questions guaranteed to get a sports-related conversation going:

- Who do you consider the greatest baseball player of all time? (Be prepared with your own answer, such as Mickey Mantle because he was so powerful as a switch hitter (he hit from both sides of the plate with his left arm and right). Throw something in like, "Did you know that the most that Mickey Mantle ever made in a season was a hundred thousand? Can you imagine that? Players now make tens of millions a season.")

- What do you think it is that makes Tiger Woods so phenomenal? (Somewhere as he answers, voice your opinion such as that his focus and concentration are incredible.

How, you wonder out loud, can he do that with such a galley of fans following him from hole to hole?)

• How in the world does Major League Baseball survive with such ridiculous salaries? (Here, you can say that the math doesn't add up with average stadium attendance and the price of the tickets. You can also point out that it has to be hard for the average family to afford an outing to the ballpark more than once or twice a month.)

• Who do you think was the greatest NASCAR driver— Richard Petty or Dale Earnhardt? (Know that both won seven Winston Cup championships but Petty won two hundred races in his career, close to a hundred more than anyone else in the sport. Earnhardt won only seventy-two. The most that Petty ever won in his career was $162,000 in one year. Earnhardt once won $5 million.)

Now, once you get in, you'll have to back it up by going to games. Don't hesitate. Jump right in there and act completely enthusiastic. And you should be, because tailgate parties are worth the trouble of sitting through four quarters of hitting and punching. Once you're completely in, it's only fair to ask him to join you on your turf for a play, a musical, or a ballet. Don't expect him to be as good at playing the game as you are. Men mean well but they have a harder time grasping our feminine interests. I once took a handsome blond football player to see *Swan Lake*. Before the ballet started, I explained the plot to him, and at intermission I reiterated.

"The evil magician has turned the beautiful princess into a swan. But every night between midnight and dawn, she turns back into a princess, and that's when the prince finds her. You know she's a swan when she is dancing with a short tutu. When she turns into a princess, she dances with long tulle that falls to her ankles."

He nodded like the quarterback he was, trying to absorb a complex new play. The curtain reopened and soon we were immersed in the magical beauty of the music and dance. After a while, I leaned over to him and whispered, "Isn't this beautiful?"

He didn't move his eyes from the stage but he nodded. "It really is," he whispered back. He waited a second and then added, "If I could *only* figure out when they're *ducks* and when they're *not!*"

Did I also mention that he was a hunter?

Linda, a smart Houston diva with more college degrees than Orphan Annie has freckles, was relaxing with me by a pool in Maui. Football season was approaching and since we had both brought the latest football magazines with us to Hawaii, we were discussing the season's prospects. Our friend Sally, a non-Southerner, slathered her perfect body with coconut oil and repeatedly tried to change the subject, bored by preseason rankings and talk of All-Americans. We ignored her and kept talking tight ends and tailbacks. Finally, she pulled herself up from the lounge and dove into the pool. Within minutes, a couple of extremely cute guys started a conversation when they walked by and saw our magazines. They pulled up the lounge that Sally had vacated and began to talk football. Perfect Sal, seeing the gorgeous guys at our side, jumped out of the pool and dashed over to join us. It was not an opportunity she wanted to miss. She assumed that her perfect body next to our imperfect ones would definitely win out. The guys were cordial and one explained that we were talking about the upcoming football season.

"Do you like sports?" one asked, trying to involve her in the conversation.

"Oh yes!" she replied eagerly. "I love the Red Sox, and I can't wait until they make it to the Super Bowl!"

Linda and I looked at each other and rolled our eyes but remained silent. "The Red Sox?" he asked. He looked at his friend and they began laughing.

"What's so funny?" Sally asked.

"The Red Sox are a *baseball* team," Linda explained. "The Super Bowl is for *football* teams."

Sally shrugged. She still didn't get the importance of it. "Well," she replied flippantly, "I'm too girly to care about sports."

"I beg to differ," the other cute guy said. "There's nothing sexier than a woman who appreciates sports."

Sally wasn't going down easily. "Well, I do love guys in tight pants. Does that count?"

It didn't. So, Sally was out and Linda and I were in for dinner with two good-looking guys who appreciate women who appreciate sports.

Rest assured, a knowledge of sports will get you far in courtship flirting. It is the most powerful tool in seducing a guy into your end zone. This is a secret that Southern women have known for years and practice as religiously as the University of Florida prepares for a game against Florida State. We had to know this in order to survive in the land of our birth. After all, the South is so taken with the rivalry of sports that the governor of Alabama is often elected on the basis of whether he played football at the University of Alabama or basketball at Auburn. Misty, a zealous tailgater, never misses a football game with her sweetie pie.

"Darlin', we Southern girls are taught at an early age about the primary religions of the South," she explains and then begins to tick them off. "Baptist, Methodist, Presbyterian, and football."

She wasn't joking.

CHAPTER NINE

HONEYSUCKLE KISSES AND BLACKBERRY COBBLERS

Liz Ann was furious. It was obvious by the way she slammed my front door. She threw her purse on the sofa and marched to the coffeepot. As she poured, she simmered.

"I just came from Daddy's house." (Incidentally, you might be a Southern woman, too, if you're over thirty and you still call him "Daddy.")

"So?" I handed her the creamer.

"His kitchen counter is covered with casseroles."

My friend's anger suddenly became my amusement. She glared as I threw back my head and roared with laughter. I knew exactly what was going on. In the finest tradition of Southern womanhood and courtship, the town's eligible women were flocking to Liz Ann's recently widowed father's abode and with them, they were bringing their best casserole dishes.

"It's not funny!" she snapped. "Mama's only been gone for two months."

"But a man's gotta eat."

"Which is exactly why I warned him to beware of any women without wedding bands bringing him casseroles." She stirred the cream into her coffee and rolled her eyes.

"Did Emma Mae take her prizewinning sausage-and-spinach casserole? The one with the secret ingredient that she always boasts about taking the recipe to her grave?" I asked curiously.

The cup stopped midway between the saucer in her hand and her mouth. "Yes," she replied softly.

"Hmm," I replied, shaking my head solemnly. "He's a goner. Bless his heart. He'll never know what hit him."

In the South, we women believe that if you can't charm him, just feed him. But if you can kiss him *and* feed him, chances are good that you'll win him. That's another trait carried over from ancient days. Men like to eat and they like their women to cook for them. Southern women are raised to cook. We know the power of a good casserole or a homemade pie. We also know that men with good mamas want to marry a woman like her. Cooking for him on a regular basis will keep him coming back and will make you stand out in a crowd of pretenders to the throne you want to own. Too many women don't take the time to cook today. That's great news for those of us who *do* cook, because it's a huge advantage in the art of courtship.

Men feel nurtured by women who cook for them. They really believe you care if you go to that much trouble, especially if you do it cheerfully. As the romance heats up and you're introduced to his family, ask his mother to share her recipes for his favorite dishes. If there's a special way that it's prepared, ask her to teach you. That woman will be your biggest advantage in winning his heart.

Food can be a very sexy component in courtship flirting. From shopping together for the food to playing together in the kitchen as you cook to sharing bites from each other's fork, it can enhance the emotional intimacy. I have always been amazed at the stories that a guy will share as he sits on a stool at the counter, sips a glass of wine, and watches admiringly as I chop, dice, crumble, steam, fry, and bake. I think it brings back deep, joyful memories of families in kitchens and watching his mama cook. Like a hot knife through butter, it breaks through barriers and removes walls so that he opens up freely and shares thoughts and stories that he normally wouldn't dream of sharing. Kitchens are very intimate, personal settings. In the South, most friends enter through the kitchen door and most heartwarming conversation is shared around the kitchen table over a cup of coffee or glass of sweet tea. Outside of the bedroom, the kitchen is the most intimate room in the house. Use it accordingly.

Flirting with Food

Too Hot to Handle

Men, whether they're single, divorced, or widowed, can be wooed with food as easily as we are wowed by flowers. Offer a man a hot meal and soon he'll be ground sirloin in your hands. Cute guy at the gym or on the subway you'd like to spend time with? Just explain how you like to cook but it's so much trouble to cook for one person. He'll take the bait; and when he does, just reel him in.

Sweethearts with Sweet Thoughts

A woman who bakes is every man's dream and will quickly earn the title of "sweetheart." She will be irresistible to men who have fond memories of their mother baking cookies. But it means even more to those who didn't. I once had a serious boyfriend whose mom couldn't cook so nothing thrilled him more than for me to bake his favorite cookies or cake. One afternoon when I took a batch of fresh-baked chocolate chip bars out of the oven, he dropped to his knees and proposed.

Many times, I have sent a date home with a Tupperware container of fresh baked goods. This is especially good in the beginning of a relationship because it ensures you'll hear from him again. He has to return your container! (Never use a disposable container if this is your agenda.) Think you can't bake? Yes, you can. Buy a box of cookie mix and dress up the batter with ingredients like coconut, a teaspoon of flavoring like almond, or butterscotch chips. Be creative. I have a cake recipe that I bake in a pound cake pan that is incredibly easy and so delicious that everyone who tastes it, begs for the recipe. Normally, I don't share it but for the sake of romance, here it is:

Incredibly Delicious, Incredibly Easy Pecan Pound Cake

1 box butter pecan cake mix
1½ cans coconut pecan icing
¾ cup oil
4 eggs
1 cup water

Preheat oven to 350 degrees. Mix all ingredients with mixer, reserving half a can of icing. Grease tube pan and dust lightly with confectioner's sugar. Then pour batter into pan. Bake at 350 degrees for one hour. Cool cake in pan for about 15 minutes. Frost top with remaining half can of icing.

Recipe for Success

If a relationship stalls or he's taking too long to call and ask for another date, a home-cooked meal is the perfect excuse to call him. Southern women still have a lot of old-fashioned ways about us and that makes it a bit uncomfortable for us to call a guy and ask him out on a date. Southern men, for the most part, still adhere to the man picking up the tab so if we call them and ask them for a date, they'll plan on paying. Thus it feels rude to call a guy and ask him out so that he can spend his money. Inviting a guy to dinner at your place solves all that. It gives you an excuse to call him, a chance to reciprocate for the money he's spent on you, and the perfect opportunity to impress him. It's courtship flirting at its most perfect.

Finger Foods

Is there anything sexier than having a luscious guy nibble food from your fingers, especially when he nibbles a finger as he takes the last crust? I don't think so, either. Handled right, your heart and his will be pounding rapidly. It is incredibly alluring and flirtatious. So make certain you have a lot of finger foods around when he comes to visit.

COURTSHIP KISSES

Women, particularly young ones, tend to give away too much on the first date and in the beginning of a relationship. Those women would find it more beneficial to rein it in and play more discretely. Not just because a woman gains more in a relationship but also because she retains more of her self-respect. Several women have told me that sleeping with a guy on the first date, one who never calls again, deteriorated the respect they had for themselves and made them feel lousy. *Don't allow anyone to take your self-respect.* Why give even a modicum of it to someone who hasn't earned your respect yet? There are many problems with becoming intimately involved with someone early in a relationship. Let's look at a few.

It Gives Him the Upper Hand

Pure and simple—guys can have sex and walk away from it. Women can't. We're usually too emotional and sensitive for that. Once we've gone that far, we're invested emotionally, and that reshapes our strategy. In fact, it blows strategy out of the water because we are no longer negotiating from a position of strength. It's very important in the game of romantic acquisition for a woman to maintain the emotional and intellectual upper hand.

It Steals Respect

If you're too easy to conquer, it erodes the respect he had for you and hampers his respect from growing. *Remember: Men are hunters.* They like the chase. It appeals to their sense of adventure and ego. If it's too easy, they're not interested. Let me put this in terms that a Southern woman understands. We adore high heels. If I find a lovely pair of heels that is quite affordable, I buy them immediately. If I find an expensive pair like Giuseppe Zanotti or Manolo Blahnik that I love, I don't snap them up. Instead, I dream of them for a while, all the time saving my money to buy them. When I make the purchase and they're mine, they mean a lot more because of the effort that went in to acquiring them as opposed to the reasonably priced ones that I was able to buy immediately. The Zanotti and Blahnik shoes in my wardrobe are cherished and adored much more than the others. In other words, I don't have the respect for the cheap ones that I have for the hard-to-get ones.

Men Talk

When it comes to sex, men are the worst gossipers in the world. They can't wait to tell the other guys who they've bagged. Again, it's the hunter mentality: They are natural baggers-then-braggers. Most social circles are pretty tight, which means this information will be shared with other prospective dates. Then, you're in a no-win situation because if you date any of his acquaintances, they expect the same thing. It can become a never-ending circle that leads nowhere, and that doesn't help foster a relationship with the guy who started it all.

Diminished Pride

We Southerners are a terribly proud bunch. It isn't always a good thing, but in this case it is. You need to feel good about yourself so that you'll be confident. Confidence is what will make you successful in whatever you start out to do. If you sleep with someone who then doesn't call you back, how will you feel? Like dirt. Know how good and confident you feel on those days when your hair is perfect, your makeup is flawless, and you have on a cute outfit? It's equally important to feel as good on the inside so conduct yourself in a manner that will make you feel that way.

The beauty of courtship flirting is that it's coy, alluring, and emotionally but not physically seductive. It's designed to keep the guy's interest there and to sustain that interest until he so flat dab in love with you, there's no running away from it. For your sake, his sake, and the sake of enduring romance, play it smart.

SMOOCHING STRATEGY

Courtship flirting calls for putting your foot on the pedal and holding it at a half-throttled position. This takes practice because our impulse is to lay the pedal to the floorboard and go full speed ahead. Don't. Remind yourself that while it feels awkward at first, it will pay off with a little patience. Remember, too, that when guys hand out speeding tickets, they tend to revoke the license, which means we're never in the driver's seat with them again.

Let's take an in-depth look at some perfect flirtatious kisses for courtship.

Honeysuckle kisses—This beautifully flirtatious kiss is used when standing across the room or sitting across the table. Deliver a flirtatious remark then playfully kiss the air, add a jaunty wink, turn around, and walk away with an exaggerated wiggle. Like the honeysuckle that fragrances a summer day, the kiss will hang in the air and cling to his imagination.

Fingertip Kiss—This is one of my favorites. I use it to punctuate a flirtatious comment. Kiss the tip of your forefinger then snap it forward as though you are putting a period on the end of an imaginary sentence.

Kisses flitting through the air—Is there anything sexier or more flirtatious than a kiss blown through the wind? A beautifully manicured hand lifted to rose-colored lips that gently touch the fingertips before lightly flittering away and sending the sensuous kiss floating through the air toward its handsome intended? As the tender kiss leaves the fingertips, a flirtatious smile and wink spells *sexy* in capital letters. Guaranteed to melt resistance and win hearts.

A kiss on the cheek—This is very appropriate for the end of a first date. Plus, it's one of the sexiest tools of courtship flirting. Cheek kissing is playful, especially over dinner when you're sitting together in a booth—not across the table from each other—sharing food and nuzzling your forehead against his cheek. A light kiss on the cheek is tantalizing. Being stingy with kisses in the beginning stokes the fires of passion. Fires of passion that are started slowly, using flirtation as the kindling, burn hotter and longer. It's human nature to want something more when there's been a long, savoring period of anticipation.

A kiss on the hand is still continental—A man who makes a woman feel like a lady will feel more like a man when she finishes with him. To entice a man to kiss your hand, reach over and squeeze his hand playfully during a flirtation moment. Drop your head, glance up coyly through your lashes, and smile coquettishly. Almost in a trance, he'll probably lift your hand to his lips and kiss it gently. This Southern-style aphrodisiac will titillate both of you. It's fun to kiss his hand, too. During a moment of hand-holding and eye gazing, lift his hand to your mouth and kiss it softly, never taking your eyes from his. It's potent stuff. I once watched as a seventy-year-old friend kissed the hand of a gentleman caller from her hospital bed. It was so sweet and perfect and, in an age-appropriate way, it was sensuous.

No kisses on a first date—Especially if you just met him a few hours before. Southern women are excellent at bringing someone close where they feel warm but still drawing the line that keeps flesh separated from flesh. This is where the intrigue for him begins.

Embargo on French kisses—Be slow to give these because once you enter that territory, it's a short, star-lit stroll to being over the moon. To stay in control of a flirting situation, you have to stay in this orbit. Remember the goal of flirtations is to get him to fall in love with you before he tastes the pralines.

Madeline Grace and Bobby Lee were high school sweethearts who parted company for college. He went to Mississippi State and she went to Ole Miss, creating divided loyalties that could put a serious strain on any courtship. Folks always said that if their relationship could withstand four football seasons of that rivalry, then they were born to die together.

So after college, they tied the knot and lived happily for several years. Then, one day, word came to Madeline Grace that Bobby Lee was sharing kisses with another woman. This came from a reliable source though a disreputable character—the other woman herself. When Bobby Lee arrived home that night, he found his clothes and fishing rod piled out on the lawn. No amount of whimpering, denying, apologizing, or begging could get Madeline Grace to open the door. Finally, Bobby Lee left, but continued to plead his case on a regular basis. A few weeks later, during a stormy phone conversation, Madeline Grace burst out with, "Bobby Lee, you can just kiss my ass!" Then she slammed down the phone. Madeline Grace, a Sunday School teacher for little ones, made no apology for her language since everyone knows that *ass* is a Biblical word.

About thirty minutes later, Bobby Lee was cooing at her front door. "Oh sweetie, I'm heeeeeer!"

She flung open the door. "Whatta you doin' here? I just told you to kiss my—"

"I know!" he exclaimed gleefully. "That's the first time you've offered to let me kiss you in a month! I'll be happy to start at the bottom and work my way up!"

That, of course, is what could definitely be called "kissing up."

Seductive Flirting

CHAPTER TEN

LURING HIM IN WITH SWEET ALLURE

Men can't resist women who are sweet and feminine. It attracts them as surely and as quickly as bees to the fragrant smell of magnolias on a warm spring day.

My friend Maggie readily admits that "I'm not all that much to look at but I make the most of what I've got and it works." No truer words have ever been spoken. I've seen Maggie at parties where beauty queens—and beauty queens are plenty in the South where pageants are taken as seriously as presidential elections—were no match for her allure and charm, both of which team together to make her an unforgettable woman. Maggie is never without a devoted man while there are many others waiting in the wings. Once a man falls in love with her, he never gets over it.

How can that be?

Simple. Maggie makes a concentrated effort to be an ultra-feminine woman and to make the guys around her feel like ultramasculine men. She powders, perfumes, and prepares herself to perfection each day. She relies on feminine necessities like provocative high heels that show her legs—skirts and dresses dominate her wardrobe—glossy, eye-catching hair, brightly colored manicured nails, appropriate makeup, and sexy lingerie. "Sexy does as sexy feels," she points out. Absolutely. *When a woman is confident and feels sexy, she puts out a seductive sense that draws men like flies to honey.* It isn't overt sexuality but subtle sexiness. Quietly and effortlessly, it draws men like hound dogs following the scent of a fox.

GOOD SENSE FLIRTING

While making the transition from courtship flirting to seductive flirting, remember a simple rule of thumb: *A great flirt has the good sense to use all five senses.* Because men tend to be more analytical than emotional, they are drawn by what they can actually see or touch. A smart flirt asserts herself by using all that is naturally at her disposal and enhancing it when necessary.

Sight

Men are extremely visual. They are first drawn to what they see, so dress for him. *Remember: There has never been a man who didn't love to see a woman in high heels. Wear high heels on the outside and sexy, matching lingerie on the inside and you will turn any man inside out. That's a promise.*

Color magnetically pulls men toward you. A pop of bright color will whop 'em upside the head in a way that'll make 'em see stars for days. Once, dressed in an eye-catching hot-pink suit, I was walking up Fifth Avenue in New York. Several men complimented me on my suit as they passed, throwing out comments like "Great color!" "Beautiful!" and such. While I was stopped at a crossing, one well-dressed man stepped up beside me and said, "That is a stunning color. What do you call that? Fuchsia?" I laughed flirtatiously, winked playfully, and said, "Actually, I think the proper name is raspberry." He chuckled. "Well, it certainly looks beautiful. Nice to see. I get so tired of seeing women in black all the time." He walked on and I looked around. On both sides of Fifth Avenue, it was a sea of black. Women were swimming in it (and some were drowning in it). Then, I realized why so many men had been drawn to me that they had complimented me. In a bright color, I stood out in the crowd.

Smell

Nothing is more powerful as an aphrodisiac than a woman scented in a lovely fragrance. Spray your hair. (it holds scent longer than skin) and dab your neck so that when he leans over to kiss you, he'll smell the loveliness, which he'll always remember as uniquely you. When he leaves to go on a trip, scent a handkerchief in your fragrance, place it in a plastic bag, and send it with him. He'll love it and he'll long for you while he's gone.

Touch

From smooth, moisturized legs and pampered skin to cashmere clothing, silk gowns, and satin sheets, give him the feel for all things luxuriously feminine. Men love to touch a woman who feels soft and sensuous.

Sound

Compliment and coo. Brag, don't nag. Laugh, don't yell. These are the most pleasant sounds a man will ever hear. It is a natural tendency to move toward pleasure and away from pain. When a person complains, argues, and nags, other people, regardless of how strong the love is, move away. Instead, use your soft feminine voice to draw him close.

Taste

Champagne, home-cooked food, and you. It's all he'll ever need.

IT'S ALL ABOUT YOU

Winning the heart of a certain guy is all about how you feel about yourself and how you conduct yourself. Even the hardest, coldest heart can be melted over time by an irresistible woman who uses social flirting and is confident in who she is. Shakespeare said, "Rain wears down marble." That can be you—soft, sweet rain that patters away on the hard surface of his heart until it's worn down and won. You've gotten him past the courtship flirting stage so, if this is the one you want, get down to the business of winning him completely.

Have Complete Confidence

Men love women with confidence. It draws them like a magnet. But remember not to be cocky or arrogant. That completely turns them off. Always behave as though there were still things you have to learn and that you want to learn them from him. Sometimes it's a fine line; but they want women who are soft and somewhat vulnerable but not needy.

Don't Be Intimidated by Other Women

Oh boy. Guys don't like it when we're bothered by other women. It throws off an internal alarm inside that warns them to stay away from someone who is jealous or intimidated. Sure, relationships can last for a while like this but they will not endure forever. One day I realized that I hadn't heard from a close male friend of mine in several months. So I shot off a very innocent, short e-mail asking him to let me know how he was doing. I received a terse reply that had, apparently, come from a girlfriend. She answered, saying, "Lance is doing fine. He's engaged and getting married in a couple of months." I couldn't believe it! A female who was opening her boyfriend's e-mail and answering on his behalf. It was incredible to me so I responded, "Please have him reply to me." She wrote back, "Please stop e-mailing my boyfriend." It is sad to see someone so insecure. Women who do these things suffocate and eventually strangle the life from their men. It is the best way to run a man off. Guaranteed.

Want Him More Than You Need Him

Initially, some men may be drawn to "needy" women, but that gets old quickly. It's like a chigger burrowing into a man's flesh. It will bite the heck outta you and just keep biting until it dies. An undeniable appeal of Southern women is their independence tempered with a seductive vulnerability that pops up from time to time. Men enjoy knowing that a woman chooses him for the person he is, not the money or security he can bring to her life.

Be Strong—Stand Up to Him

Southern women are not mealymouthed. We have opinions and aren't shy about stating them. Men (and women, too) are drawn to interesting people who have opinions and don't always go along nicely with what others have to say. Men like a certain sassiness in their women so find your voice and don't hesitate to use it.

Project a Pleasant Disposition

All people are drawn to others who make them feel soothed and comfortable. If you aren't a talkative person, smile a lot (even a shy smile will do) and always treat him with kindness and thoughtfulness as if he is the most desired person in the world. Beleaguering him signals that he is an adversary. If he brings out the worst in you, which causes you to treat him differently, have the courage to end it; you're causing yourself as much pain as you're causing to him. It's just not worth the grief.

Greet Him Warmly

No matter what your day has been like or even if you're annoyed with him over something, smile brightly and make him feel welcomed. Too many snarls or grimacing welcomes will eventually drive him away.

Smile

A smile is worth a thousand words. Enough said. Aside from a gorgeous red teddy, it is your most important accessory.

Play the Name of the Game

Use his name a lot . . . as long as it's sweetie, precious, baby, honey, sweetheart, or darling.

Talk Is Cheap, But It's Priceless

A good conversationalist can keep a man utterly spellbound. Men normally don't like to talk a lot, but when they do, they appreciate a woman who can enchant and entertain with words. It's a skill well worth cultivating.

Listen

The greatest, kindest compliment you can ever give to a man is to listen. Look into his eyes, connect, and get into the moment with his story. Nod, ask questions that demonstrate an interest, and be encouraging with your words such as, "That's a terrific story. Thank you so much for sharing it with me." In today's world, everyone gets beat on a lot so a bit of attention is one of the kindest things you can offer. It will draw him closer to you. Always take the time to show interest in what he's doing and ask about it. Even if he mumbles a short answer, he will take notice that you asked.

Compliment

Know how you feel when someone brags on you? That warm, exuberant feeling? Men like to be bragged on, more than any woman you ever met. You cannot do this enough. Stroke his ego, and he'll stroke your hair.

Make Timeless Treasures

Take a moment to send a note or e-mail that will lift his spirits. Watch his favorite television show with him. Go to a luncheon with him that features a (boring to you) program that interests him. Men love for us to suffer with them.

Humor Him

Never underestimate the power of a sense of humor, particularly when it's self-deprecating. Especially when you've bumped up the car or burned the dinner.

Be Loyal

No matter what happens or how he acts, always back him up publicly. If you disagree, do it in private. Men, being the military-like creatures they are, love loyalty. Give it to him in force.

Give Him Space

Here's yet another difference between men and women: We think that the closer he is to us, the more he loves us. He thinks that he can love his woman just fine by going a few days without calling or seeing her. Like most women, this drives me nuts. But I know that nagging about it will push him further away and, most important, it will chip away at my self-esteem in the relationship. Groveling, in any form (unless you've screwed up and need to repent sufficiently), is unhealthy.

Create Moments

Not all precious moments in time just happen. Some need to be created. Ever notice in Hollywood "feel good" movies how they put romantic characters in places out of step with modern times—places like fairs, swimming holes, picnics under large oak trees? Try it yourself. There's a lot to be said—and remembered—about lazy, sweet, quiet moments. Make them come to life.

FLIRT ALERT:

Teach him how you want and expect to be treated.
The best a man will ever treat you is in the
beginning of a relationship. It doesn't get better. If
you're not pleased with the initial treatment,
changes have to be made. Either by you or by him.

The most attractive quality about a woman is her self-confidence, which leads to a wonderful inner peace that underwrites her personality and how she treats others, especially the man she loves. Be aware of this and don't, under any circumstances, give this away. Sometimes in relationships, there comes a time when you have to draw a line in the concrete. One that cannot be erased. When a man is taking you for granted or bruising your esteem, put on your highest heels and click away as fast as possible. Stay gone, too, until he comes looking for you. I promise he will, because men can't stand to be cast aside. They hate it worse than we do! They always come back to women who don't crawl and don't cry wolf. I've had to do this with a couple of guys that I loved deeply but there was no other way. I prefer being alone than being neglected. I warned them strongly many times but when I walked away, I walked away resolutely. I didn't call, despite the worse urges. I thought of them constantly, but I stayed strong, and it worked because overcoming temporary weakness will bring permanent strength. Once, one called me back, and I took a couple of weeks to return the call. In my youth, I wasn't as wise. I caved in and called with my first love. He came back but we could never get the relationship on an even keel where I felt right again. We were doomed.

To lure him back with sweet allure, remember to be sweet—no ugly words, mean messages, talking bad about him to his friends—and walk away gently with no big scene. This doesn't mean you can't lay it on the line to him about his behavior and firmly tell him that you will not be treated that way. Just do it in a nice, ladylike manner. Then wait. And, sometimes, you have to wait and wait. Normal recovery time is a month. Sometimes it's shorter and sometimes longer. But, just as surely as the strong, bold Mississippi River roars toward the sea, he'll be back. When he comes back, you'll be equal partners or, in the best-case scenario, you'll have the upper (pretty little manicured) hand. That's what we like best!

Don't ever forget: The absolute best way to lure a man with seductive flirting is to be sweet, charming, and—always—hard-to-get.

CHAPTER ELEVEN

RULE THE ROOST,
BUT PAMPER THE ROOSTER

The firmest rule of seductive flirting is to spoil your man until he is reduced to a pile of soft grits. Baby him, and your slightest whimper will be his heart's command. Fussing over him like he's a baby will send his manly urges soaring through the roof of a three-story Tennessee plantation house. That's because detailed attention is an irresistible force, akin to that of a hurricane hitting New Orleans. It will knock him down and sweep him away.

FLIRT ALERT:

*To be an outstanding seductive flirter, you have
to first excel at social flirting.*

The South is a gracious society filled with hospitality, delicious food, friendliness, and lovely women who are feminine feminists. We rule the roost, but we pamper the rooster. As a result, he struts around proudly with his tail feathers poking straight up, convinced that he is in charge and encompassed with the warm feeling that he is thoroughly and decadently loved. Over the generations, Southern divas have perfected the mysterious art of coaxing life and love into our well-manicured, delicate fingers. Part of that mystery lies in charm, seduction, and a deceptively gentle tenacity; but another part lies in the tradition of babying our men. It isn't the cadence of our lyrical drawl that entices men into our aura of splendid charm. It's irresistible femininity mixed with a complete willingness to coddle and nurture our men. It's the art of making them feel special and so good about themselves that they are compelled by you and yearn to be in your presence. It's seductive flirting.

As discussed earlier, we use many of the same flirtatious techniques in both personal and professional situations. But when it comes to our men, we take the toe of our Giuseppe Zanottis or Jimmy Choos and kick it up a bit. We simply add more sizzle in the bedroom than we use in the boardroom. It's a key to success in society—seduce with the power of charm, graciousness, and femininity.

FLIRT ALERT:

It's extremely gracious to let a man think he's the boss until the time comes when he needs to know he's not. Sweetly letting him have his way most of the time will enable you to have your way when it really counts.

Once, I was a guest on the morning show of an all-sports talk radio show in Atlanta. I was there to promote a new book that revolved around the time in my life when I was a sports-writer, but after about five minutes of talking about that book, the guys switched to talk about my previous book on the al-lure of Southern women. We chatted about the importance of lipstick and mascara when one of the tough jocks asked, "How do Southern women treat their men?"

I laughed and then winked. "Like precious babies. We spoil them silly. I always say, 'If he wants a bowl of ice cream, *get up and get him a bowl of ice cream!*' "

Cheers went up in the studio, and one of the handsome jocks with perfectly sculpted muscles took my hand, fell down on one knee, and proposed promptly while the radio audience listened. Another, whose girlfriend (later his wife) is a true-bred Southern woman, spoke up. "That's exactly what my woman does. She takes care of me like that, and I am a very happy man, as you can see."

That studio was electrified as I explained that I have never felt that I compromised my womanhood, my feminism, or my independence by catering to the needs of a man and answering his whims and desires. On the contrary, I believe it enhances my womanhood because I feel I am genuinely giving of my-self to someone who has a piece of my heart. After all, most women do have that nurturing gene that needs to be exercised. Besides, in the South, we're raised to be gracious hostesses to those in our homes. Why shouldn't that graciousness be ex-tended to the one who sits or sleeps besides us? I would never tell anyone who was sitting on my sofa and wanted something to get up and get it himself. Consideration and graciousness like that doesn't make me less of a woman, it makes me more of a person and more desired as a lover.

No sooner were those words out of my mouth, than every light on the phone was blinking rapidly. The first caller was a woman who took issue with my advice. She whined. (Who likes whiners?) "Why does a girl have to wear makeup? I think I look cute in my baseball cap and I never wear lipstick."

The guys rolled their eyes and shook their heads. One spoke up and cut straight to the chase. "Where are you from?"

"Boston," she replied in a tiny voice.

Another jumped in with his advice. "Look, if you don't want to play by our rules then go home!"

I almost fell off the chair laughing at that "our" business. See, none of those guys was born in the South but like most non-Southern men, when they found themselves in the bosom of Southern womanhood, their hearts found new homes. The calls that came in after Miss Boston were all men, enthusiastically endorsing my assessment. Many were involved with women with similar philosophies, while others wanted to be. By the time I got home, I had received more than a dozen e-mails through my Web site from men who wanted to date me, marry me, or just worship me from afar. I was open to all three options.

Bless their hearts, men need women like us. For all that manliness and tough business, they're little boys who just want to luxuriate in the spoils of our good graces and red lingerie. And, bless the hearts of the women of the South, we know how to give what it takes.

A friend of mine is married to a man who is a Southern sports legend. He's tough with a no-nonsense demeanor, which has played a dominant role in his success. His wife, though, is bubbly, outgoing, attractive, feminine, and one of the best storytellers you will ever hear. Born and raised in Alabama, she is the most perfect example of Southern womanhood that you could ever meet. One day over lunch, I asked her how she dealt with her strong-willed husband. I knew she had a method because they have been married for decades. She set down her fork, squared her shoulders, and looked at me straight in the eye without flinching.

"It's simple," she replied. "I just go along and let him have his way until it's something that's important to me. Then I draw the line." She folded her arms and lifted an eyebrow seriously. "And believe you me, he knows not to cross that line!"

Don't forget that men deal mostly in logic and reason, whereas we deal in primarily in emotion. So a typical man will reason that since he gets his way most of the time, it's fine to let his female counterpart have her way on occasion. Of course, we all know that the majority of the rest of the time when he thinks he's getting *his* way, he's actually getting *our* way. We're just smart enough to let him think he was smart enough to think of it himself.

THE DELICATE TECHNIQUES OF RULING WHILE PAMPERING

Indulge

You have to baby the sweet thing. Let him watch the ball game if that's what he wants. You can read or needlepoint or gaze adoringly at him. (Commercials are for making out so just be sure that you get your own time-out.) If blue is his favorite color but not yours, hide your dislike by wearing a dress in that particular hue. Let him have a night out with the boys. Take advantage of the time to go out with the girls. Make his favorite recipe at least once a month and look the other way when he eats a big piece of chocolate cake, though, heaven knows, his waistline doesn't need it. It's these kind of treats and pleasure that make love special.

Adore

Claim the role of head cheerleader on his team. Find the good things he does and point them out. After we've been in a relationship for a time, there's a tendency to criticize while overlooking words of congratulations. If you're not careful, both of you will start believing the worst in each other. Don't let that happen. Always look for the good and speak it loudly into his ear.

Ignore

Don't listen when others, including your mama, criticize him. He's your man, so stick up for him. This is something that men love even more than sex. They're used to being the defenders so when a beloved woman steps in and does it for them, it's downright orgasmic. Also, ignore little things about him that aren't perfect. No one is perfect, including you. Focus on his good traits and celebrate them fully.

Endure

Men are never going to treat us perfectly. It's not in their genetic makeup. It's impossible for them. First of all, they suffer from a lack of memory. They can't remember when exactly they're supposed to call, when your birthday is, or what day your first date was on. This is not a problem that is specific to one man. It is a general problem of the gender. Learn to cope and endure. It is possible to make it better but you will never fix it. Beating him up on it repeatedly will succeed only in driving him away from you. If you can get him to do well 75 to 80 percent of the time, you are, as we say in the South, stepping in high cotton.

Keep Him Feted and Sated

A man well fed in the dining room and bedroom will treat you to any dessert or delicious treat you little ol' pea picking heart desires. *Remember: You've got to eat, too, and who doesn't need loving?* Just work it to your common good, and you will have him trailing behind you like a devoted man servant. He'll be happy and, most important, you'll be in charge.

One of my Mississippi friends is the best at pampering her husband. She does so to the point that he is spoiled rotten. She has this beautiful way of cajoling him when life is tough or work is rough. She cooks a delicious dinner every night and—now this is really something—she crawls out of bed before dawn every morning to make breakfast and to pack him an elegant, gourmet lunch. This is very minor to all the other things she does, such as making sure that his assistant knows to stay away if he's in an ornery mood and answering every little whimper and whisper. She isn't a pushover, though. When a situation calls for her to be tough with him, she does. She doesn't hesitate to go toe-to-toe, eye-to-eye with him. Because she's so wonderful to him all the other times, he may grumble but he always gives in.

This particular rooster treats his cherished chick special in other ways, too. I was having dinner with them one night when he proudly talked of how well his wife of many years treats him. He bragged on and on, a sparkle dancing merrily in his eyes. Then, he concluded, "I treat her well, too. Because she makes my life so pleasant, I want hers to be pleasant, too. I let her spend whatever she wants to and I never say a word about the credit card bill. No matter how big it is."

Her large blue eyes widened, and she exclaimed—her first words during his entire spiel—"Yes, but precious darling, you *know* that I never spend over fifteen thousand a month."

Now, *that's* what I'm talking about.

CHAPTER TWELVE

The Fine Art of Winning His Heart with Red Silk and Black Lace

Men melt to a puddle of testosterone for a woman who wears beautiful lingerie, especially if it's sexy. They don't even have to *see* it to be seduced mentally and emotionally; they just have to believe that you're the kind of woman who adheres to this sexy, extremely feminine policy. Such knowledge will drive them nuts and, eventually, straight into your arms. Isn't that always the objective?

Since this is a favorite sermon of mine, reporters often interview me about it, including a nationally syndicated columnist who wrote a wordy feature using quotes from me, such as "I've always been told that beauty comes from the inside but I say that beauty comes from the underside" and "Dress like you never know when it's coming off." I also made that last comment on national television, which caused my rather prudish mother to take to her bed for a few days. Nonetheless, the syndicated column ran in my hometown newspaper one

Friday and, apparently, was read with great interest by the male population—especially the Baptists. On Sunday morning, I showed up at church and was practically ambushed by single men. By the time I arrived in my customary seat on the twelfth row, I had fielded requests for three dates.

The following week, the pastor called to ask if I would give the offertory prayer that Sunday. Immediately, I thought of the column and was embarrassed to think of walking the aisle while folks thought of what they had read. Without explaining, I tried to beg off, but he persisted so I agreed. Sure enough, after church on Sunday, I found myself surrounded by folks, mostly bachelors, who leaned over and jokingly whispered, "Do you match?"

"You should be ashamed!" I teasingly reprimanded one. "This is a time for sacred thoughts."

"Oh, trust me," he replied with a wink, "I consider these to be very sacred thoughts!"

This goes to prove, of course, just how important garter belts are in the Bible Belt. We're passionate enough to sing our hearts out for the Lord in the choir on Sunday morning and passionate enough about life that we hope He's looking the other way on Saturday night.

I appeared on a talk show where the female host was curious about Southern women's propensity for beautiful lingerie. "What is this about your lingerie? Southern women match their lingerie?" she asked. My mouth dropped. I was shocked. After regaining my composure, I asked, "*You mean you don't?*"

How could that be? Matching underneath is just as vital as matching on top. When you wear sexy lingerie, you feel sexy. When you feel sexy, you act sexy. It's that simple. It's an undeniable fact of romantic flirting as it strolls toward seductive flirting. After all, flirting is about having fun *and* getting your way.

FLIRT ALERT:
___

*A man's mind can always be changed by a
woman who changes into something sexy.*

Many well-rounded Southern women attend liberal arts colleges where they are schooled in many life-enriching skills, knowledge, and philosophies. But professors never lectured on the most important art of womanhood—tantalizing the opposite sex with sumptuous lingerie. There is nothing more devastatingly divine to a man than matching undergarments and gorgeous silk gowns that slide so sinfully sweet against satin sheets. This is seductive flirting at its most pulsating, highest heart-throbbing level. This is the kind of flirting that segues from fun and games to the mating game where the hunter claims his beautiful trophy and she claims triumph. Southern women love the prettiness of this game because we firmly believe that sexy is as sexy feels. If you feel sexy and beautiful, your behavior reflects that and men respond accordingly.

THE DOWN AND PRETTY OF IT ALL

Beautiful Thoughts

Think yourself beautiful. Unfortunately, too many women think themselves ordinary or unattractive, and they become

that. We tend to see every wrinkle, pound, or flaw. Those negative reflections build up like shampoo residue, taking the
glossy shine from our eyes and complexion. Dulled by it, we
truly aren't as beautiful and seductive as we can be. Even when
it's hardest, I work resolutely to practice beautiful thoughts.
Think over and over, "I am beautiful. I am desirable" until it
sinks deep into your subconscious. Too often, women rely on
others to boost their ego through compliments. It's easier,
quicker, and more powerful to do it yourself.

Beauty Treatments

Take time to treat yourself well. Toss away that worn-out
T-shirt or sweats that you wear to bed and start wearing
pretty, comfortable gowns. Even when no one else sees them.
After a bubble bath followed by a skin-drenching of lotion,
nothing feels prettier than to pull a silk gown over your body.
It's also a nice way to wake up in the morning when you can
run your hands over silk or satin.

The Sweet Smell of Romance

Many women who take the time to wear fragrance spray it on
before heading out the door. There's nothing wrong with that,
because seductive flirting is always enhanced by a glorious
smell. Personally, the strongest aphrodisiac for me is a man
who wears cologne. Men feel the same about us. Get in the
habit of dabbing it on before heading to bed. You'll enjoy it
and he will, too. Spraying your pillows with a fragrance is also
a delightful idea. Also, if you take the time to layer the fra-

grance—lotion, powder, perfume—it'll last longer and you'll feel more pampered by the little extra attention you give yourself.

Sexy Shavings

If you're not in the habit of shaving your legs daily, get in the habit. Men love to run their hands repeatedly over smooth skin, especially on the legs. No man wants to make love to a porcupine.

Sitting Pretty

When you cross your legs, don't flop the top leg down. Keep it lifted slightly above your other thigh, which creates a slimmer, sexier look. Also, take plenty of time to sit in his lap, always allowing one breast to brush against his chest or arm.

The Perfect Match

A romantic coupling that is perfect begins with bras and panties that match. Please don't wear a black bra with white panties. If you do, look in the mirror and see if it's visibly pleasing to you. Hopefully it's not and you will realize that men feel the same way, too. Men loovvvvve matching lingerie. Good for them. (Especially when they pick up the bill for it.) Who would want a man who wants a woman who doesn't match?

I was doing a television show in Louisville on which viewers were invited to call in and ask questions. One young woman called in and explained that she had been married for seven years, had two children and, though she and husband were only thirty, their sex life had become almost nonexistent.

"How can I change that?" she asked in a pitiful voice. "He doesn't seem to have attraction for me anymore."

I knew immediately what the problem was and that it was an easy fix. I knew it was so easy that I asked with a big grin, "What do you wear to bed? You're not wearing an old T-shirt or sweats, are you?"

Silence for a moment. I started to laugh. I knew she was having a hard time with the confession. Finally, in a tiny, meek voice, she said, "Uh, yes. I wear one of his old T-shirts. I've worn it so long that it has holes in it."

"I thought so!" I replied while the host started giggling.

"But it's so comfortable," she wailed. "And after a hard day with the children, I just want to be comfortable."

"Well, you can be comfortable *and* sexy. Listen, there's no time to waste. You need to get thee to the lingerie store immediately. Today."

To her credit (and his credit card), she listened because she cared deeply about what happened to her marriage. I got a note from her later that said that she did as instructed and it changed everything.

"My husband wanted to write you a note and thank you personally but I told him that I'd write it. We feel like we're on our honeymoon again. You were right—the gown is just as comfortable as the T-shirt plus I feel prettier and sexier."

SEDUCTIVE STRATEGIES

Southern women know that seductive flirting calls for the use of props. In the beginning of a relationship, setting the scene for an evening of romance is fun and folly. It's easy because love and romance are new. Gradually, that changes and what was once delightful fun turns toward being a chore. Use mind over matter here and remember that very little matters more than being in love and having that strong, healthy relationship. At the start of the heart's romantic trail, you're eager to do the list of things that follow. So eager, in fact, you'd like to do them every night. Don't burn yourself out. Savor them like a box of exquisite chocolates that takes a long time to devour. In the art of seductive flirting, you must keep the mood light and the atmosphere ignited with surprise. So strive to have a night of meaningful romance one to two times a month using the following tips. These, of course, are meant to be coupled with other seductive flirting techniques that I've outlined, which should be implemented daily.

Smoke and Mirrors

A girl's number one best friend in igniting a blaze of desire are scented candles. They smell lovely, glow beautifully, and create a lovely ambiance. In the soft light, romance is mirrored in each other's eyes.

Giggles and Bubbles

A scented bubble bath shared by two, along with candles, wine, and soft, romantic music will unite your spirits and bathe you in anticipation of what is to come.

Satin Sheets

Nothing is more sensuous against bare skin than sleek satin. It's decadent and irresistible. Don't save these but rather use them every night. To both of you, they will feel better than a pair of closely shaved legs.

Perfect Planning

Southern hostesses always put a great deal of thought into planning an event. Treat a night of seductive romance the same way. Spend a few days or even a week to plan out your flirtatious seduction. This not only ensures a wonderful happening but it builds your anticipation and excitement—like a child waiting for Christmas.

Fresh Flowers

Nothing perks up your bedroom or spirits like a bouquet of fresh flowers. It's so special. Today, it's easier and less expensive than ever to treat yourself to fresh flowers. It's not unusual to get two weeks' worth of fresh floral beauty out of a few dollars. To make your flowers last longer, change the water often and trim the stems when you do. A plain old aspirin dropped into the water punches up the staying power, too.

Scent Sense

While fragrance is innate to romantic senses, be mindful to blend the scents of perfume, candles, and flowers. Lavender is soothing and romantic, though in the South, we have a special place in our hearts for magnolias and honeysuckle.

Tidying Up

Do this around the house—and around those special, intimate places, too. Bikini waxing is a good friend to romance.

Chocolate-dipped Strawberries

So pretty, so easy, and a nice prop for flirtatious teasing. Feed those to him, kissing in between bites.

Music to the Ears

You want him to hold you close and whisper words of love and romance. Enhance those words by choosing romantic music. Nothing is lovelier and more gentle than Gershwin, Sinatra, Dean Martin, and other golden voices of decades ago. Unless, of course, it's a contemporary singer who is cooing those heart-moving standards.

Time Is of the Essence

Slow down, take your time, and revel in each other. It is hard to find anything sexier than gazing for a long, quiet moment into each other's eyes.

Protect Your Feminine Mystique

Close the bathroom door for personal business. Cover up with a towel when you get out of the tub. Then let it drop seductively. Less of you in these ways is always more—more appealing.

Fun and Feisty

Even though seductive flirting is the most serious type of flirting, it's still important to keep it lighthearted and playful. You'll enjoy it more and so will he.

Remember: To be a good seductive flirt, you have to first be a good social flirt. Once you've become comfortable with flirting in the mildest form, you'll find it easy to high-heel kick it up to the truly potent stuff that is pure passion. Flirting, in any form, should be practiced until it is done with ease, until you aren't even aware of what you're doing. It should flow through you naturally with delight and good humor. And when it does, you are certain to be delighted and good humored by the results.

WEEKEND DIARY OF A FLIRT

Flirting works. It really does. It makes lives more pleasant—yours *and* the people touched by your smile, sparkle, and spunk. To illustrate the potency of feminine flirtation, the following is a diary of a typical weekend of flirting that occurred when I flew from Atlanta to Cincinnati, Ohio, for a speaking engagement. None of this was planned or manipulated for the purpose of this diary. It all occurred naturally. Halfway through the weekend, I realized that the events would provide a picture-perfect illustration of the art of social flirting, so I began to record them.

Friday, 3:00 p.m.

The crowds at the Atlanta airport are brutal. It is a holiday weekend. The train arrives to speed passengers to their various concourses. A massive crush of people jam the train, taking all the seats as well as the poles and hand straps that hold you steady during the jerky starts and stops. I push my way onboard, followed by a handsome young man with dark wavy hair, light olive skin, and large brown eyes. Our eyes meet briefly, and I smile in a friendly manner. He pushes his way over to my side. He looks down and smiles as the train prepares to leave.

"You can lean on me to keep steady," he offers.

I look up, a bit coquettishly, through my lashes and smile. "Thank you." His arms are sturdy, massive from weight lifting. I lean against him and am, in fact, quite steady against his heft.

"Where are you going?" he asks.

"Cincinnati. What about you?"

"Toronto. It certainly is busy today."

"Incredible," I reply. "I hate it when it's this busy." I look him directly in the eyes and smile again. "I'm getting off at the next stop. Concourse A."

His eyes flicker with pleasantness. "Me, too!"

Flirtatiously, I smile and give a slight flutter of my eyelashes. "That's very good! Because if you weren't, I bet you would be lonely without me for the rest of the ride." My tone is teasing and playful.

The train jerks to a stop. He laughs, now moving into the full swing of playful flirting. "You're right! I would be!" He steps back to allow me to exit in front of him. I stop outside the train and wait a second for him to catch up.

"I'm going to gate twenty-nine," I offer as we step onto the escalator.

His eyes widen happily. "I'm going to thirty-one! We're going in the same direction so we can walk together."

"What a happy coincidence!" I smile broadly and lightly touch his bulging bicep with the tip of my fingernail. I pause because "a moment" is beginning to occur. It is a time when words would destroy everything. We look at each other for a moment, then I shyly glance away and then back up at him. He is staring at my hair.

"You have the most incredible hair."

I laugh appreciatively and respond teasingly, "You know, I *thought* I was having a good hair day!"

He throws back his head and laughs. "Well, you were right!"

We walk through the concourse, chatting. We discuss our occupations, and he tells me that he works in wireless communications and satellites.

"Oh!" I squeal, genuinely delighted. "I needed you last week when I was trying to learn to use this new wireless gizmo I have for e-mails. I still don't know how to operate it."

He smiles. "Well, when I come back, why don't we get together for dinner and I'll see what it'll take to make that little gizmo work."

We stop at my gate and continue flirtatiously chatting, then exchange cards and part company.

What Happened and Why It Worked: His attention was first drawn my way because I was wearing bright, vibrant colors and was dressed to stand out in the crowd. While others were dressed in black or in jeans and a sweatshirt, I was wearing a pumpkin-orange suede jacket and melon-colored sweater. The colors initially captured his attention. Too many people dress for flights like they dress for yard work. If you want to attract people to you, you have to stand out in the crowd. Then I smiled at him when he boarded the train. I made myself approachable. I also looked him directly in the eye, which demonstrated that I was open to conversation. He felt comfortable enough to speak to me, and I responded with friendly chatter. The conversation moved from simple social flirting to more of a romantic flirtation when I used humor and a teasing tone. *Remember: Flirting should always be fun and light-hearted.*

Cincinnati Airport, 6:00 p.m.

A nice gentleman from the rental car company picks me up in the shuttle. I am the only one on the van so I make pleasant chitchat on the drive. He instantly responds and begins to give me directions to my hotel and other helpful information, such as where to eat and what streets to avoid. We arrive, and both of us step out into the cold, blustery wind. He runs over to open the door for me and says, "While you check in, I'll go and get your car for you!"

"Oh, you don't have to do that," I protest.

He smiles. "Glad to do it. I'll be right back."

I am finishing up the paperwork when he comes in. He gets out a map, writes down all the directions, and points out which exit to choose when I return. He walks out with me and I discover that he has loaded my luggage and turned the heat up on high to warm the car for me. I shake hands with my new friend and tip him (please tip well to people who are kind. It's one of the loveliest ways to put goodness back into the world.). Again, I thank him for his kindness that made my travels more pleasant.

"Thank you so much for customer service, above and beyond the call of duty." He smiles happily and I feel warm all over despite the chill.

What Happened and Why It Worked: Social flirting, in its purest form, treats everyone equally. It makes others feel good about themselves and about you. I treated the driver of that shuttle bus with the same respect that I would give to the pilot of a jetliner. I talked to him and respectfully listened to his opinion. I even wrote down the suggestions he made for dinner. For a man who is probably ignored by most passengers, it was an uplifting experience. To show his appreciation for that feeling, he went out of his way to do something nice for me. It wasn't planned on my part, but the simple truth is that people mirror our treatment of them. Kindness is met with kindness. That's one of the great pleasures of social flirting.

Hotel, 6:30 p.m.

A pretty young woman is checking me in. I notice her fabulous chestnut-colored hair with golden highlights. It is glossy, and the light bounces off it beautifully. As I hand her my credit card, I remark, "Your hair is absolutely gorgeous. The highlights make it stunning." She looks up shyly and smiles sweetly. "Thank you," she replies. We begin a conversation on hair as she is tapping on the computer.

"Nonsmoking king?" she asks.

I nod. "That's right." When I booked my room earlier, I had opted not to take a room on the river because the price was 20 percent higher. Since it's Friday evening and they know how many reservations they have, I decide to ask for an upgrade.

"Are you completely booked tonight?"

She shakes her head. "No."

"Is there any way that you might be able to upgrade me to a river view?"

She smiles. "Let me see." She taps away. I don't say another word about it and neither does she when she hands me my key. When I get to the room, she has upgraded me to a suite with a river view. The room was fabulous and the view was gorgeous. Immediately, I call downstairs to gush and thank her. I ask her name, and then I fill out a glowing comment card on her, which I later deliver to the front desk (again, when someone is kind to you, return the kindness).

What Happened and Why It Worked: From the moment I arrived, I was friendly. I saw something that was stunning about her and complimented her on it. I was sincere. Southern women love hair, and we know beautiful locks when we see them! This is definitely our area of expertise, which probably made her feel better, knowing that an expert was bragging on her. Nonetheless, she responded with kindness to my kindness. Then, I responded to her kindness with more kindness. A cardinal rule of flirting is that you can't take without giving appreciation. You know how we Southern women are about thank you notes!

Local Restaurant, 8:00 p.m.

I have dinner with a friend at a quiet restaurant. The waiter's name is Justin. Each time he comes over to fill our water glasses or to bring something, I look up and thank him while smiling at him. He is a college kid and he's sweet and earnest. I make a tremendous effort to acknowledge him and compliment him on his service. As a result, we receive impeccable attention from him. He even surprises us with a piece of "complimentary" cheesecake. When the evening ends, we pay the check and have more discussion with him. We learn that he is a sports journalism major and since I was once a sportswriter, I hand him my card and tell him to e-mail me with any questions. "I'm happy to help you in any way," I say. He grins from ear to ear and promises he will.

What Happened and How It Worked: Again, social flirting at its best. My friend and I both strived to make a young college student, who was waiting tables to work his way through college, feel important. He responded by providing us the best service possible and giving us a piece of cheesecake. Social flirting opened the door for me to see the goodness in him, which led me to offer my help. The most beautiful part of social flirting is that it gives you wonderful new friends that you would not otherwise have.

Saturday, Hotel Restaurant, 7:00 a.m.

The breakfast buffet line ends with a stern-faced woman who is cooking omelets to order and dishing out the sausages and bacon.

"Good morning!" I say cheerfully.

"Mornin'," she replies sharply.

I begin a conversation. I talk about how skilled she is at omelet making as I watch her toss the ingredients together and make a perfect omelet. I ask questions. "Do you have to work this early every day?" She begins to loosen up and talks about work and her schedule. Finally, a bit of a smile tugs at her lips.

"What else can I do for you?" Her tone has been de-iced and is now warm.

"Do you have any bacon that is fried crisp? I only like bacon that's crisp."

She chuckles and winks. "Me, too." She hustles off to the kitchen and returns with a plate full of perfectly crisp bacon. She hands it to me and leans over to whisper, "This is from a special stash I've got back in the back. Only nice people get this bacon!"

Her sudden warmth makes my day. I thank her profusely and leave.

What Happened and How It Worked: Again, the cardinal law of social flirting—treat everyone with warmth and kindness. A woman who has to get up early and travel in the ice (it had snowed and iced over night) just to make omelets for others deserves that warmth and kindness. She wasn't in a good mood but a bit of effort turned her mood and helped reset the tone for the rest of the day. To reward my flirtatious courtesy, I got the best crispy bacon possible.

Hotel Restaurant, 6 p.m.

I return from a speaking engagement and go straight to the restaurant for dinner. I am well dressed in an eye-catching, monochromatic beige outfit. The waiter, a young man, comes over to get my drink order.

"Will someone be joining you?" he asks.

"No." I smile.

"You're so dressed up to be by yourself. Nice outfit. Very pretty."

Now, I move into flirtation mode. I tilt my head and look up through my lashes. I smile coyly. "Thank you. You're so sweet." Men like to be called sweet. In fact, men like to be bragged on, period. You can never do enough of it.

He comes back with my drink. "So, your husband won't be joining you?"

I laugh. I know this drill. "I don't have a husband."

"Boyfriend?"

"No."

Playfully, he sits down quickly across from me at the table and says, "So, what are we going to do tonight?"

"*You* are going to take my order and then bring my dinner." I say it teasingly and he laughs as he hops up from the chair. Sassiness—always in a playful tone—works well in such situations.

Later, after dinner, I ask if I can sign it to my room. His eyebrows shoot up. "Yeah! Then I'd have your room number!"

"On second thought, here's my credit card." I wink to take the edge off of it and he laughs. Harmlessly, we flirt a little more when he brings back my receipt for signature. I leave feeling very good about myself because a cute, younger man has seen fit to flirt with me.

What Happened and How It Worked: The first step is to enter a room and catch attention with the way you dress. I was dressed conservatively yet trendy. Another necessity is well-groomed hair that is glossy. Southern women like to be the center of attention, so we know how well that good hair attracts others to us. (You, too, could have Southern blood if one of the worst days of your life revolved around something that happened to your hair.)

With the young waiter, I flirted back but kept it on an appropriate level and did it in a way that did not belittle him. I smiled, winked, and teased. And when I left, I walked a little taller because his social flirting made me feel more beautiful and sexier. See—social flirting can benefit you, too!

Sunday, Cincinnati Airport, 11:00 a.m.

I sit down three empty seats away from an airline captain deadheading it home. Later, as we're waiting to board, he approaches me with a smile, and I smile back to show he is welcomed to speak to me.

"Have you ever seen the movie *Scent of a Woman*?" he asks.

I shake my head. "Al Pacino, right?" He nods. "No, I've never seen that movie but I have wanted to." I pause for a minute. I know this is headed somewhere. "Why?"

Again, he smiles. "I was sitting over there, my eyes closed, almost asleep, when you sat down. The fragrance of your perfume drifted over, and I woke up."

"Oh no!" I exclaim. "Is it too strong?"

He shakes his head adamantly. "No, not at all. It's very lovely."

We begin a conversation of social flirting and by the time we board the flight, we've become fast friends.

What Happened and How It Worked: The pilot was right. The fragrant scent of a woman is incredibly alluring. Too many women fail to wear perfume these days but those who do, enable themselves to stand out in a crowd and attract men. Again, a smile and eye contact encouraged him to approach me. I responded with chitchat. It's an important skill. Learn how to talk about nothing and make it sound interesting. Simply put, be approachable and smell good!

MD-88 Aircraft Somewhere over Kentucky, Noon

I began flirting with a male flight attendant.

"I'm so sorry to bother you," I begin when I approach him in the galley. My body language says I am definitely flirting. I tilt my head, look up through my lashes, clasp my hands and hold them close to my chest, and, of course, smile very sweetly.

He grins back. "Well, you are bothering me." He winks. "What can I do for you?"

"Could I please have a bottle of water?"

He smiles again. "You can have two." He gives me the water. I thank him and head back to my seat while he prepares to serve the rest of the cabin. Since it is a short flight, they are offering express service, which means passengers are allowed to choose among only three beverages. Of course, none of the three is what I want. The male flight attendant stops at my seat. Again, I smile and slightly flutter my lashes.

"When you finish with the service, is there any way that I might have a cup of coffee?" I look hopeful.

"Black?"

"Cream, please?"

He nods and smiles as he hands me a bag of pretzels. I shake my head gently. "Do you, by any chance, have those wonderful little cookies?" I purse my lips in a sweet little pucker.

He can't help but laugh. "I think I can find you some." Later, he comes back with my coffee then a couple of minutes later, reappears with two handfuls of cookies and drops them on my tray. I tilt my head, look up through my lashes, and smile beatifically. "Thank you so much! You are so sweet!" I say it with all of my heart and mean it. Meanwhile, all the other passengers look around and wonder why I have a beverage and cookies not offered to them. Of course, I was still bragging on him when I deplaned.

What Happened and How It Worked: When dealing with men, feel free to pull out all the stops—flutters, winks, smiles, light touching, humor, and bragging. They love it and will crumble like a fresh-baked buttermilk biscuit into your hands. Men can never get enough bragging so just remember: Brag, don't nag. Flutter, don't stutter. Wink, don't blink. By becoming an artist at flirtation, the world becomes a canvas that you can paint to suit your own sweet self.

FLIRTING AT A GLANCE

Top Rules for Social Flirting

1. Do whatever it takes to strengthen your self-esteem and keep it healthy. You can't make others feel good about themselves unless you feel good about yourself.

2. Be gracious, kind, and thoughtful to all. In Southern speak, "Be real nice."

3. Stay well-versed about many subjects so that you can say a little about a lot. This helps you to demonstrate interest in others and what they have to say.

4. "Please" and "thank you" should be used regularly, and thank-you notes should be part of your normal routine.

5. Learn to tell a great story. You can't be a great flirt without being a good storyteller.

6. Embrace humor and be willing to laugh easily. Laughter unifies.

7. Employ "charmnacity" by persistently charming others—even the mean ones—until you win them over.

8. Play professional matchmaker by introducing acquaintances who you think could do business together. This kind of generosity will be rewarded in unexpected ways.

9. Flatter others by finding things to compliment about each person.

10. Shake hands firmly, hug when appropriate, and don't hesitate to invite others into your personal space.

Top Rules of Courtship Flirting

1. Men are natural-born hunters. They're most intrigued by women who are hard to capture.

2. Don't be overly available, especially if he is moving slowly and cautiously. Attempts to speed up the relationship will slow it down and cause trouble and emotional suffering.

3. Be a good sport. The typical guy loves sports, which makes him more likely to love the woman who loves sports, too.

4. Never call a guy after a first date. Let him call or let him go.

5. If a guy kisses you passionately but doesn't call for forty-eight hours, keep your distance emotionally. Oth-

erwise, you'll be flirting with a heartache. It's easier to nip a little heartache in the bud rather than to allow it to grow to a full pulsating, tormenting level.

6. Practice charmnacity. If you're charming and tenacious, you will eventually get the one you want. Make certain, though, that you really want him before you launch a charmnacious approach, because it works!

7. Don't underestimate the maternal influence. Enlist his mother as an ally. Together, you'll win the war.

8. Don't smother him. Encourage him to have an evening or afternoon with his pals or to go hiking by himself.

9. Give him your complete loyalty and support. Even more than sex, this is what every man wants.

10. Make him feel good about himself and he'll feel good about you.

Top Rules of Seductive Flirting

1. The best seductress feels confident and has a healthy overall self-image. It gives that important edge for successful flirtatious behavior.

2. Make him feel good about himself. Encourage him and don't nag. Nothing diminishes a woman's sex appeal more than a nagging tongue.

3. Be gentle, soft, and alluringly feminine. Men find it hard to resist a feminine woman.

4. The bedroom is no place for a power struggle. It is a time for coming together as equal partners. So, don't use sex as a bartering tool for things you want. Or, even worse, don't withhold it as a punishment. This sets up a psychological whammy that, in the long run, takes the fun out of what should always be a joyous experience.

5. Pamper him. If he wants a peanut butter sandwich, make it for him. It doesn't compromise you but strengthens the relationship. A well-behaved pampered man will return the favor. If he doesn't, dump him and find one who deserves you.

6. Men are visual creatures who are first attracted by sight. For a night of fiery romance, make him see "red," as in nightie or teddy.

7. Fragrance is an incredibly powerful aphrodisiac. Smell good and it'll make him feel good and he will then, in turn, make you feel good. Sound good?

8. Use all five senses to intensify your allure and the experience.

9. Observe other women, both those who are in healthy and thriving relationships and those who aren't. Learn from both because patterns of success and failure repeat. Women who cherish, adore, and enjoy their men are in happy situations while women who nag and ignore them and cease to take care of their own personal appearance are in unhappy ones. Look, listen, and learn.

10. Maintain the fun of intimacy. If you ever let it stray over into the area of a chore, it's hard to steer it back to being fun again.

Must-Haves for a Modern Flirting Girl

1. A subscription to *Sports Illustrated*—perused weekly, left out in the open on your coffee table, and always carried on planes.

2. Season tickets to something that involves rules and balls.

3. Sexy high heels.

4. Shimmering lip gloss.

5. Chat maker—something you wear, carry, or possess that will encourage the start of a conversation.

6. Magnetic smile—smile big and often. It'll draw others to you.

7. A cheerful, bright-colored coat or jacket—to stand out in the crowd.

8. Eye-catching hair—long, short, blonde, red, silver, dark, or curly. Hair is the number one thing that catches a man's attention. Make sure that yours shines.

9. Starter story—guys have it, you should, too. Develop a line that leads into a story and gives you reason to walk over and talk. In a store, pretend you're looking for something and say to a cute guy, "You look like just the guy who can help me!"

10. Smarts—if you don't have 'em, get 'em. Read and stay current on daily events and pop culture.

Top Places for a Flirting Girl to Meet Guys

1. Home-improvement stores—The more bewildered you look, the more offers to help from male shoppers you'll get. (Be sure to stop by when you're dressed up and have heels on. It draws men to you like flies to honey.) Even if you rent, you need lightbulbs and batteries. Buy them there.

2. Ball games—They're so simple, but so often overlooked.

3. Civic clubs—Community-oriented, ambitious guys belong to these. What more could you want? Also, volunteer for charity events. Help others and help yourself at the same time. After all, charity begins at home.

4. Bookstores—Particularly on rainy Saturday afternoons. Taking a peek at what he reads helps you to read him.

5. Lecture series—Enrich yourself. Hopefully in more ways than one.

6. Sports bars—Guys go in groups, especially on weeknights. Take a group of girls and form tag teams.

7. Airports—Lots of guys traveling alone. Check for a ring (or tan line) then take a seat and strike up a conversation.

8. Churches and synagogues—Pray and prey.

9. Concerts—Don't stay home and sing the blues. Buy a single ticket on the evening of the event. You may be surprised who'll you meet in line doing the same.

10. Grocery stores—Single people have to eat, too. Find them on Aisle 9 in the "Dinner for One" section.

A Flirting Girl's Secret Weapons

1. Matching lingerie

2. Charm

3. Femininity

4. Wit

5. Sports savvy

6. Seductive perfume

7. Storytelling brilliance

8. Three-edged razor (for the smoothest legs possible)

9. Satin sheets

10. A great wink

Flirting Girl Don'ts

1. Never relinquish your power.

2. Don't give up too much too soon.

3. Never wear a white bra with black panties (or white shoes *after* Labor Day. But then you knew that, right?)

4. Don't forget to ask about his mama. Then ask for an introduction.

5. Never aggressively pursue him; always do it subtly.

6. Don't be caught low on thank you notes, lip gloss, or perfume.

7. Don't talk about old boyfriends.

8. Don't take discourtesy, inconsideration, or abuse.

9. Never mind the negatives; focus on the positives.

10. Don't be catty—personally, professionally, or socially. Instead, be kitten sweet.

What Guys Know About Savvy Flirting Girls

ACKNOWLEDGMENTS

This book is the sequel to a very successful first book and for that, gratitude is owed to Richard Curtis, agent, John Duff, publisher, and Sheila Curry Oakes, senior editor, as well as the publicity staff headed by Liz Perl. Without the first, there wouldn't have been the second.

And for the second, I am appreciative of the efforts of many: Jane Dystel, Miriam Goderich, and Michael Bourret of Dystel-Goderich Literary Management; Sheila Curry Oakes, again, who bought *What Southern Women Know About Flirting* then broke my heart by changing publishing companies; John Duff, who resolutely believed in and fought for this book and his brilliance in hiring my new, energetic editor, Marian Lizzi. Laurie Cedilnik, Craig Burke, and Miss Liz Perl all tossed their expertise and assistance on the table and were fabulous. I love working with all of you.

Additionally, I owe thanks professionally and personally to

Travis Massey, master photographer, Jim Whitmer, Sam Richwine, Barclay Rushton, Mary Eaddy, Virginia Stanley, Edithe Swensen, Loretta Tucker, and Rudy Corn.

Personally, I am blessed with a loving and supportive family, including Mama, my siblings, and all the rest of the relatives. I am, though, especially indebted to Mama and Louise because their antics supply this storyteller with terrific material. A woman never had more good friends—especially those who are good examples of flirts—than I do. Many are already recognized in the book but I am especially grateful to Karen, Debbie, Nicole, Sharon, Kim, Chantel, and Myra, as well as the entire gang of Dixie Divas. Thanks for the inspiration and the friendship.

And, finally, to all the newspaper editors who are kind enough to carry my syndicated newspaper column. While each publisher is very important to me, I must thank Brian Blackley for being the first to courageously step forward and sign up for the column and to Norman Baggs, Johnny Vardeman, Alma Bowen, and Phil Hudgins for being terrific journalistic mentors.

I am so blessed to have you all in my life.

Speaking of blessed, I truly am. Thank you, Lord, for all the prayers you have heard and answered.

ABOUT THE AUTHOR

Ronda Rich is the author of the popular *What Southern Women Know (That Every Woman Should)*. In her first novel, *The Town That Came A-Courtin'*, she writes about a small town in search of a wife for its widowed mayor. It is based on a personal experience.

She is an eleventh-generation Southerner who firmly believes that charm disarms. In her weekly syndicated newspaper column, "Dixie Divas," she writes humorously and poignantly of the South and its women. Ronda is a popular speaker who delivers humorous, inspiring presentations. For more information, please visit her Web site, at www.southernallure.com, or e-mail her at southswomen@bellsouth.net.

Ronda, who lives in Gainesville, Georgia, is a daily devotee to the fine art of flirtation.